Healing

for our Soul Gardens

Restoration and Wholeness After Sexual Abuse

Healing
for our Soul Gardens

Restoration and Wholeness After Sexual Abuse

Kristin Clouse, MA LMHC

REDEMPTION
PRESS

Published by Redemption Press, PO Box 427, Enumclaw, WA 98022

Toll Free (844) 2REDEEM (273-3336)

Redemption Press is honored to present this title in partnership with the author. The views expressed or implied in this work are those of the author. Redemption Press provides our imprint seal representing design excellence, creative content, and high quality production.

ISBN 13: 978-1-68314-303-1 (Print)
           978-1-68314-304-8 (ePub)
           978-1-68314-305-5 (Mobi)
Library of Congress Catalog Card Number: 2017941031

Acknowledgments

"Other people are going to find healing in your wounds. Your greatest life messages and your most effective ministry will come out of your deepest hurts." —Rick Warren

I love how God's Word tells us "He refreshes and retires my soul (life)" in Psalm 23:3 (AMP). God truly has done an amazing work in my life over the past twenty-nine years since I accepted Jesus into my heart and life. Restoration for myself and others has become my lifelong passion as I have ministered in the various roles God has used me in over the years.

My husband, Rick, has been an amazing support to me over the years. He was the one who held me when I cried and comforted me when I was working through the healing process in my own life. He has been my biggest fan and support as I have transitioned from the broken, to the restored, to the one who helps the wounded. For him I will always be grateful and cherish his love and support.

My children, Kaitlyn and Ross, are a testament to the power and restoration of God in my life and I feel so honored to be called mom, mother, or yo mama by them both!

In my life I have been very blessed to have an amazing support system through my healing process and as I have transitioned to one who walks with others through their healing process. Three people have been "my people" - my go to people for many years and their love, support, prayers, encouragement, and belief in me has been a gift. They have seen who I was in Christ, before I even realized it and I am forever grateful for them. Sandy and Bob Prosser, mom and dad, have been spiritual parents to me and have loved and spoken life into my dry bones when I didn't see who I was or could be in Christ. Janet Brown has been a friend, a sister in Christ, whose friendship and love I will always cherish. I truly believe that Bob and Janet are celebrating with me as they are in heaven with Jesus.

I am grateful for those who have helped me in this writing process. Sandy Prosser and Debbie Justice, who read each chapter as I completed it. Your support, wisdom, and input were so valuable during the writing process. For my editors, Barbara Todd and Marlene McCurley. What a blessing you both were to me in each season of writing this book!

Finally, I am thankful for God's presence in my life. Without Christ I would not be the woman of God I am today. I am truly blessed by God's love and faithfulness. To turn this broken vessel into a restored treasure is beyond what I could imagine! To God be ALL glory, honor and praise!

With Love, Kristin

Contents

PART 1

Introduction

This book is a story of restoration, healing, and new beginnings. This is a journey I have taken, and my prayer is that you will find healing and restoration as I did. This path is not easy, but it is necessary that you take back your life and no longer be a victim of what happened to you. When I first began the healing process, I often wondered if a day would ever go by when I wouldn't think about my experience. Would I ever be normal again, or would I forever be marked by the negative experiences I've had? Now, I don't think about it every day. I am as normal as I can be, if that's possible. (My friends can attest to that one.) And even though I am marked by what happened to me, it does not define who I am and what my purpose in life is.

The intention of this book is not so much to tell the story of what I experienced but to share the healing process I went through to find my life again. It is my hope and prayer that you, too, will go on this journey and find the wholeness I believe God has for you as well.

For the past few years, God has been speaking to me through the analogy of comparing my life to a garden. I love to garden. In my early adult years, I did not have a green thumb, nor was I a master gardener. I knew little about gardens, which may have been more symbolic than I realized at the time. As the years have gone by, I have learned to love and understand gardening. I have found so much joy and rest in my time in my own garden. It has become a place where my creativity flows. I have savored the moments when my hands are in the soil, and I am at work creating. It is in those moments that God speaks to me in His kind, gentle way and talks with me about my own garden, my soul, and of the work He has done to restore me to the garden of life He created me to have. This is the journey I would like you to take with me. It is a journey of healing, revelation, peace, understanding, newness, forgiveness, and beauty.

1

How It Began

I remember the details. They are as clear to me as if it were yesterday.

It's about six o'clock in the morning, and I am walking down the street. Tears are coming down my cheeks, but I feel numb and oblivious to what is around me. So many emotions are going through me at one time, and I'm not sure what to do with all I'm feeling. I'm confused, scared, and relieved all at the same time. I'm angry at my friends who left me at that house, and I still can't believe they betrayed me that way. They said they would come back; I thought they would be right back, but they never came. Did they not realize what happened to me? *No,* I think to myself, *they have no idea.* They thought I was safe. I thought I was safe. These things don't happen to people we know. This can't be happening to me again. I quickly put out of my mind those memories from a few years before. I can't allow those emotions to come tumbling out and mingle with the emotions I am now feeling.

I finally get home and immediately get in the shower. My mom and brother aren't home, so I don't have to talk to anyone about it. As I stand in the shower, I wish the water could wash away what I'm feeling inside, but it doesn't. I'm not sure how long I stand there or how many tears I shed. The water and my tears blend together and fall off my body. My thoughts keep swirling around in my mind like the water swirling down the drain. *What am I going to do?* A voice inside my head repeatedly tells me that I need to tell my mom, but I'm afraid. I know what happened to me was wrong. It was dangerous, and I'm thankful to be alive. I can't believe I survived. I pinch myself to make sure I truly am still alive and it wasn't all just a very bad dream.

By the time I'm done with my shower, I know what I must do. I must tell my mother. This means I must also tell her I lied about where I was the night before, but this weight is too big for me to carry by myself. I need to talk. I become anxious for her to come home so that I can get it out—so I can tell someone.

The phone rings. It's one of the friends who left me the night before. She asks if I'm okay. I tell her no. She apologizes for leaving me and not coming back. She says she just found out some terrible things about the guy at the house where they left me. She got scared and had to call me immediately to find out how I was. I tell her, "No, I'm not okay." I begin to cry, and then I speak the words for the first time out loud. "He raped me. He wouldn't let me leave. I tried, but then he started hitting me and threw me back onto the bed. I didn't know what to do. I was so scared that he would hurt me or even kill me."

We talk for a little bit more, and she tells me things about him that make my stomach ache. She tells me more about him, but I don't remember what else she says. Words are swirling through my head, but I am unable to process them—my mind goes blank. Everything around me begins to spin, and my body slides down the wall. I land on my kitchen floor in a heap. It feels as if I have been hit again. The tears begin again, and I struggle to breathe. I can't talk anymore and quickly get off the phone.

The rest of the day is a blur. All I know is that I need to talk to my mom. When she finally gets home from work, I try to talk to her a few times, but then I walk away, shaking. Finally, I call her into the bathroom and with tears running down my cheeks, I tell her everything. She's shocked but immediately takes me into her arms as I cry uncontrollably. I was worried about getting into trouble for lying to her, but she says it doesn't matter. She just comforts me and speaks words of encouragement into my ear.

When I finally calm down, my mother gently tells me that we need to report this. I'm scared of what might happen, scared of him, but she reassures me that we need to do it. She goes to the phone and calls the police. As I stand there, I realize that my life is forever changed. There's no going back. As my mother calls the police, I wonder at what lies ahead of me.

The police come, and we make the report. I go with them to show them the house. I must tell them everything that happened and everything he did to me. I am humiliated and embarrassed as I quietly speak to them. One of the officers reassures me that I did the right thing when I stopped fighting him. He tells me I am lucky to be alive or not physically hurt worse, and it was due, in part, to how I handled the situation.

The officer, and later, the district attorney, reassure me that they would not release my name and that the details would be kept confidential. However, word got out, and the knowledge of what happened invaded every aspect of my life. Everyone at my school and throughout our town found out. Some are sympathetic, but many accuse me of lying. I am harassed at school, horrific words are written on my locker, and friends turn their backs on me.

At that time, I was a sophomore in high school, and my life was crumbling down around me. I didn't go to counseling; I just shut down and quit talking to anyone about it. It was 1981, I was fourteen years old, and everyone knew what had taken place. Those intimate details became public knowledge, and my heart became calloused to all that was good around me. Over the next few years, I turned to drugs and alcohol to find solace and peace but found nothing.

EARLIER YEARS

I was in fifth and sixth grades when my life first changed. Those years are meant for fun. We have friends, we get involved in sports and activities, and we do the school thing. I did it all and had fun, but then something happened to me during this time. It changed my fun to great sadness and confusion. I was repeatedly molested by older neighborhood kids for two years. They were from a family I dearly loved. In many ways, they had become my substitute family because I was raised by a single parent who worked hard to support

> It was 1981, I was fourteen years old, and everyone knew what had taken place.

us. I never knew what it was like to have a large extended family. They filled that gap for me.

Sadly, though, they had a secret, and I was part of it. There was sexual abuse taking place, and I became one of the victims in the line of abuse. Looking back, I can see the grooming process. I was so needy for love, and they saw that. I'm not saying their choices were my fault, but I do see that I was vulnerable to being sexually abused because of my situation.

I never told anyone about these incidents, or least I never told anyone in my family. My brother and I had a conversation years later. One day, while sitting on my porch, I briefly shared with him but did not go into details. See, I had a secret, and I was an expert on keeping secrets. I kept the secret out of fear, out of shame, and out of not knowing what to do or where to go for help. I often think that the reason I told my mom I was raped at age fourteen was connected to the weight of the secrets I already held.

As an adult looking back, I often questioned where I got the strength to walk through what I did after I spoke to the officers. My name wasn't to be publicly released; I was a minor. But it was a small town, and that is exactly what occurred. Word got out, and my friends, schoolmates, and the community quickly became the judges. I endured ridicule, name-calling, rumors, lies, and a great deal more because I stood up for myself and told what happened.

I was asked if I wanted to go to a counselor, but I didn't understand what that was, so I said no. I could talk to my friends. However, about six months down the road, one friend came to me as the spokesperson for the rest and said that they thought I was bragging because all I did was talk about it. It wasn't until years later that I learned my desire to talk was part of the process of working through the trauma. I just went to the wrong people with it. Those words hurt me, confused me, filled me with shame, and were the catalyst to the path I followed over the next seven years.

Obviously, there was something wrong with me, or so I thought. I was dirty, not worth anything, and definitely not likable or wanted unless I played by someone else's rules. These thoughts and so many more plunged me into a lifestyle of drugs, alcohol, and promiscuity. I pushed my hurt, pain, and feelings deep down inside. I put them in a trunk, locked it, wrapped it with chains, and locked the chains. I put the chained trunk in a room deep inside, shut the door, and barricaded it so that no one could get to that part of me, not even myself.

Does this sound familiar to you? Is this similar to what you may have done? It wasn't until I was twenty-one years old that I began to make the steps, at a slow pace, to take my life back once again. It was at this point that I became a Christian, and shortly thereafter, I became pregnant with my daughter. Still, I was filled with hurt, pain, anger, pain, confusion, pain, uncertainty, and yes, even more pain. It was overwhelming. It was unbearable, but I had come to a decision that what I had experienced was no longer going to define me. I was no longer going to live my life as a victim.

I made a choice to fight for my life. I realized I was not created to live as a victim, overflowing with pain and too damaged to do any good in this world. I made a vow. I was going to live my life to the fullest of who and what God created me to be. I didn't want any less. This meant I had work to do. I was tired of what I had been doing before, and I was ready to move into this relationship with God to the fullest.

The journey we are about to go on in this book is about the changes that God did in me as well as my experience as a licensed counselor who works with those suffering from trauma and abuse. It's hard to narrow down all that took place in me into one book, but I will do my best. With the leading of God, I want to focus on those key points of the work He did in me and wants to do in you as well.

I've always said to people that I'm no better than they. If God can do this miraculous healing and restoration in me, then He can do the same in you. God is truly here to touch your heart, your life, your emotions, and your pain and bring you the restoration and healing you so desperately need.

> I made a choice to fight for my life. I realized I was not created to live as a victim, overflowing with pain and too damaged to do any good in this world.

I can truly say the Kristin today is who God created her to be. She is not defined by her experiences. She is a daughter of the King, the Most High. She is the apple of His eye; she is His beloved, His precious one. She is loved. She is treasured. She is accepted. She is lovely. She is created in His image, and this makes her beautiful. She was fearfully and wonderfully made. She is all this and beyond what she could imagine to be. God always knew these things about me, but I didn't for many years.

Every day, I wake up feeling blessed—blessed at where God has me and what He is doing in me and through me.

Blessed with a healthy family and children. Blessed with my wonderful church family and friends. Do I still have struggles in life? Yes, we all do, but they no longer overwhelm me, cripple me, and stop me in my tracks like they did before when I saw life through the eyes of a victim. Now I see life, the good and bad, through the eyes of one who has been healed and restored. I know what I have been through. I am a survivor. I've walked through the valley of the shadow of death, and I lived! So, too, can you.

As I have been writing this book, I have been praying for you, believing with you, and standing in the gap for you, that our God will heal your soul and restore you to who He created you to be. Thank you for allowing me to be a part of the great work God is doing in your life.

Our Soul Gardens

As you read the next few pages, allow your imagination to flow and the Holy Spirit to speak to your heart. God often speaks to me through stories or illustrations. As the premise for this book developed in my heart, God gave me a clear illustration to use as the foundation for explaining the work He has done in my life and is waiting to do in yours. Imagine with me as I paint a picture of the life God had intended for me and for you in contrast to the experiences we actually had.

I love gardens: gardens with pathways, flowers on end, stone walls, old wrought iron fences and gates; arbors filled with roses; quaint places of refuge where you can sit and enjoy the beauty and water flowing freely in fountains of refreshing life. The pathways take you on a journey filled with surprises right around every corner. The pathways are clear and defined, and even though the texture changes, they are still clearly visible. The borders show where the path gives way and the flowerbeds of beauty begin. There are rows upon rows of flowers that are mixed just right; their beauty takes your breath away. Trees of various sizes stand tall above the flowers as watchmen over the garden. At times, you need to stop and kneel to look at the flowers just below the taller blooms. These ground plants are dainty and tender, just like our spirits, and can often be overlooked if you are too busy focusing on the path ahead.

As you stand to continue the journey, your eye catches hummingbirds zooming by and butterflies gently fluttering around. You hear water and walk toward it. As you round the corner, the pathway opens wider, and a smile comes to your face as you see the flowing fountain of life-giving water surrounded by a brick pathway that leads off in many directions. You discover flowers as far as the eye can see! Off to the side, you see a pathway leading to a bench in the distance. You follow this path, take refuge on the bench, and admire the beautiful arbor of roses surrounding you on each side. The sweet aroma fills your nose; you reach over and cut one with your fingernail and place it behind your ear.

In this place of rest, you open your Bible and read words of life. You feel safe in this place. Right behind you is a stone wall, a boundary of protection and strength. There is no fear or apprehension; shame and guilt are not flowing out of your heart while you are in your garden—there is just complete peace and rest. At this moment, you see the word *selah* in the Bible guiding you to pause and meditate on what you have taken in. You stop, rest, and savor the image of what you just read. The beauty of God's creation is found in this garden and within each of us. We are this garden. We are the creation of the Master Gardener, God.

Then one day, vandals come in to your garden and destroy the walls of protection. The gates are torn down, the arbors are broken into pieces, and the statues in places of remembrance are shattered. Plants are ripped out and cast aside. By the time the vandals leave, the garden is in shambles and in desperate need of repair. The garden has been ravished, all fruit and everything of value has been stolen, and all that remains has been destroyed.

With the walls of protection gone, what was once outside is now coming into the garden, and weeds overtake the once beautiful masterpiece. Slowly, vines wrap themselves around the plants and trees that remain, destroying and choking the life out of them. Over time, pathways are no longer visible, fences are all but gone, borders are unrecognizable, and there is no clear direction or purpose to be seen for this piece of land that was once known to be an amazing garden.

It doesn't matter in which neighborhood this garden is. This isn't about gender, age, social status, education, family relationships or cohesion, or religious backgrounds. The vandals have one goal in mind, and that is to do harm to it. It is about their sexual perversion, and they give no thought about what and whom they hurt. These vandals can be neighbors, aunts, uncles, siblings, parents, other relatives, family friends, classmates, or strangers, to name a few. They are deceivers, liars, violators, trespassers, and con artists who can paint a picture of care and concern, but in reality, they bring pain, destruction, and abuse. This is what happens to those of us who have experienced abuse.

This book is written for those who have been sexually abused, but this story could apply to those who have experienced other forms of abuse or heartache in their lives. Vandals—predators—have come in, and our Soul Gardens have been destroyed. When we scan the image of destruction, the thought of hopelessness sets in, and we fear that our gardens can never be rebuilt and restored.

No Soul Garden is beyond hope. All individuals, all Soul Gardens, can grab onto the hope that is found in Jesus. In the Bible, there is a story about a woman who had been suffering from an ongoing medical condition for twelve years who grabbed the hem of Jesus' garment and didn't let go. We, too, must grab onto Jesus and not let go. With Jesus, through Him, and by Him we can begin the healing process and restoration of our Soul Gardens. My prayer is that you will begin the journey of restoration and healing your Soul Garden so desperately needs.

We have experienced abuse that has left wounds, but those physical wounds have healed over time. However, our soul wounds, our wounded minds, wills, and emotions, do not heal as quickly. Sadly, they are frequently overlooked by ourselves and others. Family and friends question as to when we will be moving on emotionally, mentally, or physically. These words add more wounds to our souls. We often put all of those wounds in a box in our hearts and lock them up for no one to see. We put masks on our faces to show that all is well. We deceive ourselves into thinking it's over, but we need to cleanse those wounds and allow them to heal just as our physical wounds healed. The Great Physician, our Lord God, is here to do just that for us.

A MOMENT OF REFLECTION

At this point we need to take some time to stop and reflect on what God is speaking to our hearts. We don't want to rush and miss what the Holy Spirit is whispering to each of us. For some, the thought of hope or restoration and healing is overwhelming, and opening ourselves to the memories and pain can be hard. Let's take a moment to pray and ask Jesus to help us through this. Remember, you are not alone. We may have never met, but I have been praying for you and so has my prayer support team.

> However, our soul wounds, our wounded minds, wills, and emotions, do not heal as quickly.

> We deceive ourselves into thinking it's over, but we need to cleanse those wounds and allow them to heal just as our physical wounds healed. The Great Physician, our Lord God, is here to do just that for us.

Lord, right now we call on You for strength, courage, and peace. God, we need Your strength to face these memories and areas that are so painful. Give us courage to face them and not close this book and walk away. We need You right now to minister to our hearts and fill us with Your presence and Your peace. We thank You that You are our strength, our hope, our peace, our everything. Where there is apprehension, we ask that Your peace would come in and fill us. Jesus, right now we grab onto You, and we are not letting go. Touch us right now, God. Begin the process to heal our hearts and heal our souls. Give us the courage we need to walk this journey and may You, O Lord, be glorified in and through our lives. In Jesus' name, amen.

WHAT IS A SOUL GARDEN?

Before we begin the rebuilding steps, we must first understand what our Soul Gardens represent. The Hebrew word for *soul* is *nephesh,* and the Greek word is *psuche.*[1] Both of these words are widely defined as *life.* To bring our definition down to a more focused interpretation: Our soul is *our minds, our wills,* and *our emotions*—life within us.

Understanding the purpose of our souls will help us understand the importance of finding complete healing back to what God intended them to be. In *The Spiritual Man* by Watchman Nee, we learn not only what the soul is, but also the original purpose for which God created it. The soul is the connection between the body and the spirit. The body represents our flesh, and the spirit represents the relationship with Christ. When our souls are damaged, the full connection to the Spirit God intended for us to have is blocked. When our minds wrongly process information or are led by intellect alone, our wills do not bow or submit to God. They are unable or unwilling to give control to anyone, and our emotions go haywire, acting out all over the place. When this happens, our flesh is growing in strength, and our spirits, our relationships with Christ are weakened.

An illustration I like to use to better describe this is to imagine there is a lamp in front of you. The parts of the lamp include the lamp base, the cord, the plug, and the light bulb. The lamp base represents our bodies, and the light bulb is what comes out of us based on the source we are plugged into. The cord represents our souls, and the plug is our spirits. If our cords are damaged, then regardless of whether we are plugged into the source—God, the Holy Spirit—power cannot get to the lamp base and the light bulb.

Watchman Nee tells us, "The work of the soul is to keep these two [body and spirit] in their proper order so that they may not lose their right relationship—namely, that the lowest, the body, may be subjected to the spirit, the highest, the spirit, may govern the body through the soul."[2]

The importance of finding healing for our souls is vital to a deeper relationship with Christ because this is where the Spirit of God is found and where we commune with Him. Our souls need to be healed; otherwise, our flesh is in control, and the connection to God, the spirit realm, is tainted by fleshly opinions, perceptions, and perspectives. It's unclean. It's not spirit-led but led by the flesh, and that is what comes out and is seen in us.

SOUL: MIND, WILL, AND EMOTION

So what is meant by our mind, will, and emotion? This is a question many of you may have. To understand our souls, we need to break down each of these parts and look at them individually to see how they affect us.

MIND

Mind represents our thoughts, intellect, reasoning, perceptions, opinions, victim-thinking, wisdom, and knowledge. Much of the work that God does in our lives is in our minds. How we interpret situations affects our emotions. Because of the abuse, our filters are distorted, and we don't see situations in our lives clearly. You are not alone in this battle of the thinking process. This is one of the side effects of abuse.

In cognitive behavioral therapy, we learn about the cognitive triangle, which involves steps to identify and reframe the thinking process. First, there is the trigger: a situation or issue that occurs. Second, the thought process creates a negative or positive opinion based on a perception of what just happened or was said. Finally, the emotions are activated based on the perspective or thought process about the situation, which are again, either negative or positive.

I have added a final step that I use when working with individuals. This is the reaction or response step. A reactor is a device used to detonate an explosive. I always think of *Road Runner*, a cartoon I watched growing up, when explaining this to individuals. Our behavior is a reaction when we are reacting to someone else's actions. The button is pushed on the reactor that detonates an explosive reaction either outward or inward. Wile E. Coyote was continually re-acting to Road Runner's action, and it always backfired on him. Reactions are based on negative thoughts and emotions.

A response is when we respond or reply as Christ would in a given situation. When we respond, we are not driven by negative thoughts or feelings. Our emotions are not making our decisions. Instead, we are replying with control, truth, and peace. Christ faced many situations while He was here on earth. His responses to others were out of love. God speaks peace in the midst of chaos and when our behavior is a response to a given situation, we, too, are speaking peace, truth, and love as Christ does. This is part of the journey where we become less and Jesus becomes more in us.

Our thought processes affect our emotions. To change our emotional responses, we need to change our thinking about what happened or how it affects us individually. This is the foundation of cognitive behavioral therapy treatment, although the Bible has spoken to us all along about the effect of what we meditate on or think about has on us.

"Finally, brothers and sisters, whatever is true, whatever is noble, whatever is right, whatever is pure, whatever is lovely, whatever is admirable—if anything is excellent or praiseworthy—think about such things" (Phil. 4:8 NIV).

"A cheerful heart is good medicine, but a broken spirit saps a person's strength" (Prov. 17:22 NLT).

"Don't worry about anything; instead, pray about everything. Tell God what you need, and thank him for all he has done" (Phil. 4:6 NLT).

"Don't copy the behavior and customs of this world, but let God transform you into a new person by changing the way you think. Then you will learn to know God's will for you, which is good and pleasing and perfect" (Rom. 12:2 NLT).

"Instead, let the Spirit renew your thoughts and attitudes" (Eph. 4:23 NLT).

Consider this analogy: Once someone experiences abuse, they put on a pair of tainted sunglasses. These sunglasses affect every situation this person views. Someone can say something to them, and they experience it through their abuse sunglasses, which causes their perspective to be off. How we see a situation affects our thoughts on what occurred and those thoughts in return affect what our emotional responses will be. Feelings of rejection, neglect, fear, anxiety, shame, or being unwanted, to name a few, can be triggered because our thought processes, our minds, have been damaged. We wear those tainted sunglasses—our abuse sunglasses—and our minds, our once healthy processing abilities, are now damaged. The good news is this: Over time we can recognize when our faulty thinking is triggered and then readjust it to line up with the truth.

This process of readjusting our thinking is found through a relationship with Christ, reading His Word, praying that the strongholds of faulty thinking would be shattered, and asking God to transform our minds into the mind of Christ by God's truth. Some of you may also need to seek counsel from trained counselors who will speak truth into your lives, not just tell you what you want to hear. We need someone in our lives we can learn to trust and who will guide us from our faulty thinking into healthy thinking.

In Psalms 13:2 (NIV) we read, "How long must I wrestle with my thoughts and day after day have sorrow in my heart?" In the New Revised Standard Version, the same Scripture reads, "How long must I bear pain in my soul, and have sorrow in my heart all day long?" This Scripture shows us that *soul* is also translated as *thoughts*.

Have you asked God the same question? Do you feel you are just like the psalmist and are wrestling day after day with your thought process? Do you have sorrow in your heart from what has happened in your life? Just as the psalmist ran to God for solace and comfort, we, too, must do the same.

Wrestling with our thoughts is something that can be overwhelming to any individual. Joyce Meyer, speaker and author of *The Battlefield of the Mind,* talks about the war that goes on in our thinking processes.[3] This war is between our distorted thoughts and the truth of God. In Psalm 26:2 (NIV) we read, "Test me, Lord, and try me, examine my heart and my mind." With the guidance of the Holy Spirit in our lives, God can reveal our faulty thinking to us. *The Message* Bible says, "Examine me, God, from head to foot, order your battery of tests. Make sure I'm fit inside and out." Our prayer to God needs to be this as well.

We need the Father to examine us inside and out and reveal His truth in our lives. This includes our thinking processes, our minds. If we rely solely on our minds and not on the leading of God in our lives, we can be led astray. Our thinking can be distorted; we can perceive situations wrongly, and our filters can be clogged with dirt, grime, and junk from our past experiences.

Our minds can also deceive us when we rely on reasoning to be our guide. Reasoning relies on man's wisdom and not on the wisdom of God. This is about faith, trust, and dependence on God. It is not easy, especially if you have been abused. With abuse comes trust issues (rightly so), a need for control, and fear based on letting your guard down. We've been betrayed, and we will not let that happen again. However, God did not hurt us. God is God. He is the one who we can trust and open ourselves, ever so gently, to find our healing and peace.

> We need the Father to examine us inside and out and reveal His truth in our lives.

WILL

Will represents our choices, our free will, our decision processes that dictate the path of our lives. When God created us, He gave us free will to make our own choices. From the very beginning, free choice was always part of the process. Adam and Eve were given a choice to follow God or to eat from the tree. Using their free will, they chose to eat the apple. They made a choice, and it changed the path for mankind from that moment forth.

Another example in the Bible of a choice that changed the path of life for two people and for all generations after them is the story of Cain and Abel. Take the time to read Genesis, chapter 4, for yourself, and then come back and join us.

Cain and Abel were brothers who both brought their offerings to God, but they did not receive the same response from God. It was said of Abel that the Lord respected him and his offering. This tells us that Abel gave his offering from a heart of worship and thanksgiving. He gave God his best.

When Cain gave his offering, God did not respect or accept it. This speaks to us of Cain's heart or soul. His will was to do things his way and not God's way. God could not respect Cain's offering because Cain did not respect God and who He was in Cain's life. Cain was given an opportunity to make things right, but he was filled with anger and instead of making things right, he blamed Abel—victim-thinking—and he chose to kill Abel. Cain's choice affected not only himself, but also his brother and generations to come.

God gave us free will because He desires to have a relationship with us that is not forced but of our own free will. God is gentle and kind and will not force Himself on us. This is a hard concept for some to understand, but truly, God's love is pure and filled with grace, mercy, long-suffering, and kindness. It's not the same love that some of us have experienced, and so it will take us some time to understand the love that God has for us.

When it comes to our own will, it is hard to let go. For many of us, it's about trust: trusting God enough to give our lives up to Him and allow Him to do the work. It is hard to let go of control especially when you have been hurt by the hand of others.

You may be thinking right now, *So, you are asking me to trust God?* Yes, I am. Trust comes in levels, and this is the first level of trust. Within each of us, there is a place we don't share with many people or for some, with anyone. This is about opening yourself to God, trusting Him enough to talk to Him and share your hurts, your disappointments, and your pain with Him. God is here right now to work through those issues in your life now or those you have hidden away that have contributed to your broken heart.

A MOMENT OF REFLECTION

I'm reminded of a song which truly speaks of letting God into our lives and have His way, depending on His will, not our own. As you sing these words, I want to remind you that you picked up this book because your heart cries out for healing. For God to begin the healing process, we need to let Him into our lives to do the work. Take a moment to spend time with God right now and sing or pray this song to Him.

All to Jesus I surrender,
All to Him I freely give;
I will ever love and trust Him,
In His presence, daily live.

Chorus:
I surrender all, I surrender all;
All to Thee, my blessed Savior,
I surrender all.

All to Jesus I surrender,
Make my, Savior, wholly Thine;
Let me feel Thy Holy Spirit,
Truly know that Thou art mine. (Chorus)

All to Jesus I surrender,
Lord, I give myself to Thee;
Fill me with Thy love and power,
Let Thy blessing fall on me. (Chorus)[4]

EMOTION

Emotion represents our feelings, desires, and affections. Just as our minds, our thoughts, can lead us astray, so can our emotions. They regulate the temperature of our souls. This is how God intended it to be for us. God created our emotions, and Jesus led by example, showing how to manage our emotions instead of letting them control us. Our emotions reflect what is happening around us. At times, they are a warning system, and at other times, they are a cooling system.

If our emotions are always hot or always cold, they are damaged. If you are not comfortable with your emotions, unable to understand them, talk about them, work through them, and face them, then your ability to process your emotions is damaged and needs healing. In a later chapter, we will take the time to discuss in greater detail our emotions and the process of learning to manage them. At this point, we need to remember that our souls consist of our minds, wills, and emotions, and thus, damaged emotions—not reading situations, people, or circumstances in a healthy manner—contribute to our damaged souls in need of healing and restoration.

PART 2

Weeding, Cleaning, and Pruning Our Gardens

As we stand here and survey our Soul Gardens, the sight of destruction can be overwhelming. At this point, our focus needs to not be directed on the whole picture of damage, hurt, or pain, but instead on what our work is for today. One of the things we notice as we observe our gardens is how weeds and vines have taken over. It's hard to see anything underneath because years of neglect gave way for the weeds and vines to gain control and take out all life.

Vines of Shame

Vines can be beautiful, and a huge variety of them can be found everywhere. For some, the vines may be considered a nuisance, and for others, they are greatly loved. Regardless of your preference, vines need to be kept under control or they can cause grave damage.

There are three types of vines that come to mind for this teaching. First, there is the morning glory vine. This is a popular plant in many gardens. At one time, in a different home, we planted morning glories. However, in the home we live in now, this plant grows wild on one side of our house. It is a nuisance, and I must stay on top of it, otherwise it will take over and choke out other plants in my garden. This plant also releases toxins into the soil that can destroy other plants around it. The root system is spread by trailers underground, and a new plant can grow from even one small piece of a root left in the ground.

This particular vine finds its strength in its leaves. The leaves store the nourishment for the next year's growth. To rid yourself of this vine, you have to remove and/or destroy the leaves, the source of nourishment. You can put weed killer on the leaves with an eye dropper or paint it on, or you can cut off the leaves continually as you see the vines grow. This requires a lot of patience; the process of destroying this plant once and for all takes at least one year. This approach is considered more thorough than going for the root. Killing the leaves, the source of nourishment, is what kills the plant and ultimately destroys the root system.

The second vine is the thorny and resilient wild blackberry vines rampant throughout the Pacific Northwest. These vines produce berries but at the cost of taking over acres of land. Wherever there is abandoned and unattended land, you are likely to find wild blackberry vines in abundance. One would think that you could mow, burn, or bulldoze these vines to destroy them, but this approach strengthens the root system causing the vines to come back stronger and multiply quicker. Trying to rid your garden or land of this vine can be very difficult because not only is it resilient, it is also covered in thorns that can be harmful to any gardener trying to cut them back.

To rid yourself of this vine, you must be ready to fight and fight hard. There are two approaches that are thought to be the best at ridding your land of this vine. First, repeatedly tilling the ground is recommended as the most successful approach. This does not mean you till the ground just once a year. The ground needs to be continually agitated, loosened up, and cultivated so that eventually what is unhealthy will be destroyed and new, healthy plants can be established. Second, using herbicides on the root system is a good partner to the tilling process.

The final vine is the ivy vine. It takes over small and large trees by growing up and around them. It attaches itself to sides of homes and gets under foundations, siding, and fencing, eroding whatever it contacts. This vine is a menace and can quickly invade and take over all in its path.

The process of getting rid of the ivy vine is the same as the morning glory. You don't want to just pull it out because if you leave pieces of the root system in the ground, a new plant will sprout up. Getting to the source of nourishment, the leaves, is how to destroy this plant. It is important to reiterate is that this particular vine can quickly and silently get into and under foundations and cause large-scale damage.

SHAME-LED THOUGHTS

Shame. We all experience it at some point in our lives. For some, however, it becomes a leading emotion in how they view life around them. Shame can rule like a cruel dictator who limits growth and truth in one's life, and much like a vine, it chokes the life out. No longer is there joy to be found. They are overwhelmed and consumed by shame. Shame has attached itself to them, wrapped itself around their source of life, and is in the process of choking them to death.

Shame takes on many forms. For those who have been sexually abused, these are just some of the thoughts that can go through their minds daily:

- I deserved it.
- I'm to blame.
- No one loves me.
- I'm not worthy.
- I'm unlovable.
- I must have seduced them.
- It happened to me because of how I dressed or because of how I acted.
- Don't tell. Keep quiet.

- It's my fault.
- I must have asked for it.
- I am not worthy of love, kindness, or peace.
- I must be gay because I was sexually abused by someone who is the same sex as me.
- Something is wrong with me.
- I should have stopped it.
- If I keep quiet, maybe they will still love me.
- If you only knew who I really am, you wouldn't love me or like me.
- If they knew me, the real me, they wouldn't like me.
- I'm a bad person.
- I'm no good.
- I don't understand how something so bad could, at times, feel good? I'm so confused.

DEFINITION OF SHAME

The *Merriam-Webster Dictionary* defines shame as:
1 a: a painful emotion caused by consciousness of guilt, shortcoming, or impropriety;
1 b: the susceptibility to such emotion;
2 a: a condition of humiliating disgrace or disrepute;
3 a: something that brings censure or reproach[5]

Shame is something we have all felt more than once in our lifetimes. Often, shame is associated with guilt, but in reality, there is a great difference between the two. Guilt is associated with an action. Someone does something they know they shouldn't, and they feel guilty. Guilt is associated with sin. Shame goes much deeper than guilt. Shame, much like the ivy vine, goes into the foundation of a person, into their core belief system, their identity, and tells them they are no good, they are worthless, and whispers lies that are destructive and damaging.

In *Helping Victims of Sexual Abuse* we read, "Shame differs from guilt in that it is not so much an emotion as it is a mindset or a perception about being a defective person. A person's identity becomes associated with feelings of inferiority, worthlessness, and self-contempt. Shame is feeling bad, stupid, inadequate, incapable, a failure, worthless, empty."[6]

We need to stop and absorb what we just read. Shame is not an emotion, as was defined earlier, but a mindset or perception believed to be true about our identities: who we are or who we are not as a person. It takes root in our core belief systems, telling us our value. These thoughts (our mindsets) then affect our emotions and feelings, confirming what we thought to be true about ourselves and our lack of value as a person. They erode our foundations of self and identity. Remember the cognitive triangle we discussed earlier in the book? This is exactly how shame works. However, much like the vines that were discussed previously, shame is one of the most difficult feelings to eradicate. It takes time, patience, diligence, a fighting spirit, and determination to do the work necessary to rid our Soul Gardens of it once and for all.

In *The Many Faces of Shame,* we read, "Guilt implies action, while shame implies that some quality of the self has been brought into question."[7] Do you believe or feel that some quality of you, of yourself, has been questioned? We need to understand that when we have these thoughts, it's shame we are dealing with, and it needs to be taken out before it totally destroys us.

In John Bradshaw's book, *Healing the Shame That Binds You,* we find, "The feeling of shame has the same demonic potential to encompass our whole personality. Instead of the momentary feeling of being limited, making a mistake, littleness, or being less attractive or talented than someone else, a person can come to believe that his whole self is fundamentally flawed and defective."[8]

> Shame has the demonic potential to encompass the whole personality. This means it causes us to believe that not just part of us, but our whole self is fundamentally flawed.

Wow. Did you get that? Shame has the demonic potential to encompass the whole personality. This means it causes us to believe that not just part of us, but our whole self is fundamentally flawed. This tells me that shame is a lie from the pit of hell and needs to be replaced in our mindsets with who and what God says we are, not who and what Satan or the world says we are.

To understand shame better, we need to go to the source, the Word of God, and find out where the concept of shame originated. In Genesis 2, we read about life in God's garden and what He intended it to be. Adam and Eve were given freedom in this garden but were instructed to not to eat from one tree, the Tree of the Knowledge of Good and Evil. In Genesis 3:8–11 we read that the serpent tricked Eve and then Adam into eating from this tree, and from that moment forth, their lives were forever changed. Let's read together:

> They heard the sound of the Lord God walking in the garden at the time of the evening breeze, and the man and his wife hid themselves from the presence of the Lord God among the trees of the garden. But the Lord God called to the man, and said to him, "Where are you?" He said, "I heard the sound of you in the garden, and I was afraid, because I was naked; and I hid myself." He said, "Who told you that you were naked? Have you eaten from the tree of which I commanded you not to eat?" (Gen. 3:8–11 NRSV)

As we read this Scripture, there are a few things that stand out in regard to shame and the power it has in our lives. First, when Adam and Eve ate the apple, their thinking processes and how they viewed themselves changed. Shame came in and made Adam and Eve ashamed of who they were. As was discussed earlier, shame is about our identity, our perspective of who we are. And like those sunglasses of abuse, Adam and Even put on sunglasses of shame. Everything from that point on was viewed through the lens of shame.

Second, Adam and Eve had always been naked in the garden; this was not something new. Every day, they walked and talked with God and each other, and their nakedness was never an issue or thought. They were content with who they were and secure in their identities. They were children of God created to have a relationship with Him, and that is what they did day after day.

When they ate the apple, they consumed the lie that said they needed to be ashamed, embarrassed, and humiliated. Immediately, other thoughts invaded their minds: thoughts of worthlessness, unworthiness, and disdain. These thoughts, mindsets, or perceptions became a part of who they were, their identities, and out of shame, they hid themselves from God.

Friends, I pray that you hear this right now: God is the one from whom we should never hide. He is here for us right now to comfort us, not to condemn us, blame us, or humiliate us. God is here to love us, to help us, to care for us, and to walk with us into health and healing, allowing us to find our true identities once again. His heart is broken for us, and He is here to heal our hearts, our Soul Gardens, and help us get rid of shame once and for all.

Finally, shame is based on secrets. Adam and Eve hid themselves from God. They didn't want to tell Him what happened. They were embarrassed to face God and be in His presence. They were afraid and ashamed, just as we have been afraid and ashamed. Carrying a secret is what we do best, but we need to understand that the root of secret keeping is shame. It's not for our benefit or protection, it keeps us in bondage, and it blocks the healing process.

THE FRUIT OF SHAME

Shame, just like a plant, produces something in our lives daily. However, the fruit it produces is harmful and damages our Soul Gardens. We need to see this toxic or unhealthy fruit for what it is so that the truth of who and what we are can set us free. Remember, shame is a mindset or perception that affects our core beliefs about who we are. As we identify the side effects of shame, we can make the changes in our lives we so desperately need.

> We need to see this toxic or unhealthy fruit for what it is so that the truth of who and what we are can set us free.

FALSE INTIMACY

All human beings have a desire to be loved. When we were babies, there were times when the only thing that would console us was being held. This desire doesn't go away as we grow up. Touch, talk, and spending time with people are all layers of intimacy. Sharing your pain and triumphs with someone is another layer of intimacy. Having a close friendship or relationship where you share your dreams and hopes of the future and spend hours upon hours just talking is vital to a healthy relationship, to one that is intimate.

There is another layer of intimacy created for a husband and wife and that is sexual intimacy. When a person has been sexually abused, a door opens that was reserved for marriage. This door opens individuals to an array of emotions, physical feelings, and stimulations that were created to happen in a healthy relationship with a spouse.

When this door is opened outside of marriage, it affects how we trust people. Mistrust and unclear boundaries cloud our interpretation of intimacy. Our understanding becomes marred and damaged.

For an individual who has been sexually abused, the journey of intimacy is a hard and treacherous road. Sexual abuse victims have been abused by fathers, mothers, brothers, sisters, uncles, aunts, grandparents, and close family friends. With this abuse comes a distorted sense of what a healthy relationship is and what it is not. The definition of love has been tainted. It becomes very common for love to be based on giving of yourself, your body, to others. If I am sexual with them, they will love me and want to be with me. It's hard to grasp that intimacy is far more than just sexual. It's hard to believe I have value as a person and that people will like me for who I am, not for what I can do for them sexually.

False intimacy can also be found in addictive behaviors. An individual who has been sexually abused is attempting to have a relationship with alcohol, drugs, sex, shopping, gambling, or food. The person is unable to have healthy, intimate relationships with another human being, so they turn to addictive behaviors to try to fill that need for intimacy. Remember, shame is at the root of false intimacy, and because of the severity that sexual abuse in particular has on a person's self-worth, they can't have healthy intimacy. Thoughts of being no good, unworthy of love, and undesirable, to name a few, are daily for many, and shame is at the root of this lie.

FROZEN EMOTIONS

Feeling emotions are difficult for those who have been sexually abused. It is much safer and doable to put all our emotions into a box, lock it, and not deal with them. We can laugh, but we are never really happy. Anger is right there on the surface, ready to stand in place of everything else that we locked away, including those feelings we can't deal with. When that happens, there are unresolved issues that pop up in other areas of our lives. However, to survive the abuse, a person quite often must numb themselves to what they are feeling. It's a form of survival. Shame tells us it's our fault. Shame leaves us with lies and confusion. Shame stunts our ability to live the life we were created to live. Later we will spend more time on our emotions and the process of unlocking that box and working through those emotions.

LONELINESS

Loneliness plagues many people. However, for someone who is dealing with sexual abuse, there is a feeling of emptiness that never seems to be filled. People from all different backgrounds experience loneliness, but the sexually abused, or abused people in general, are dealing with a cycle of trying to fill this void with wrong behaviors. These behaviors continually let us down and add to the feelings of loneliness. We will be discussing boundaries in a later chapter, but to understand the fruit of shame—loneliness—we need to touch on this subject. When no clearly defined boundaries exist regarding whom to talk to and when to talk to someone about the abuse, we set ourselves up for disappointment, which then feeds our loneliness. It becomes a self-fulfilling prophecy. We feel alone. We share details and those we share with cannot deal with the intensity of the situation. They avoid us and then we feel more alone. This happens over and over again, reaffirming our loneliness and sense that no one cares. In reality, we do have people caring about us. However, we need to learn who the safe people are and when it's right to talk to them. We need people who can process and deal with difficult information without being traumatized by it.

THORNS OF PROTECTION

When someone has experienced abuse, self-protection follows in many forms. This happens when you can't protect yourself from the abuse, so you find other ways to protect yourself from ever getting hurt again. Protection "thorns" are prickly, painful, and used as a defense against those who could do damage to us. It's easier to have our thorns or walls of protection up first before we have contact with anyone.

When abuse is happening, victims often disassociate or zone out as a form of self-protection. It's a way to live through the abuse: one more hour, one more day, one more week. It's a way to respond with flight, even if it's just within our own minds. However, once this pattern has been established as a way of protection, it's no longer limited to the abuse alone. It becomes a way of protection through any experience that causes fear, anxiety, hurt, pain, and other strong emotional feelings.

Our thorns or walls of protection become all we know in dealing with other individuals. Many can walk through life with their thorns or walls up at all times, blocking any intimacy or relationships with others. "I will reject or hurt you before you reject or hurt me." This is one of the motivations to self-protect. This fruit goes hand in hand with false intimacy, frozen emotions, and loneliness. All of these fruits fit together like a puzzle and cause great damage to the individual whose life is shame-led.

KEYS TO BREAKING SHAME

BREAKING THE POWER OF SECRECY

As mentioned earlier, sexual abuse victims are experts in keeping secrets. To think about breaking the silence is scary, intimidating, and for many, beyond comprehension. However, finding a healthy and safe person to share your secrets with is life changing.

Perhaps some of us have never told anyone or maybe a friend knows, but our parents or family members don't. Breaking the cycle of secrets takes a lot of courage, but truly, we all have the courage within us to do this. Even if it doesn't *feel* that way, we do. In Joshua 1:3–9, we read what God says to Joshua about moving forward into what He has for His people. God told Joshua three times in this chapter to be strong and courageous. In verse 9 in the New International Version Bible we read, "Be strong and courageous. Do not be afraid; do not be discouraged, for the Lord your God will be with you wherever you go." We need to grab hold of this and know that God will be with us wherever we go, with whomever we talk, reminding us we are not alone. Please hear me when I say that I am not speaking of the possibility of going to your offender to talk. This is about finding your support system and someone who is safe so you can break the power of secrecy and share your story.

> Each time we break the power of secrecy by talking with a safe person who will help us process the abuse, we are taking stolen ground back.

In verse 3 of Joshua, chapter 1, we read, "Every place that the sole of your foot will tread upon I have given you, as I said to Moses." I view this Scripture in this way: Each time we break the power of secrecy by talking with a safe person who will help us process the abuse, we are taking stolen ground back. Not only are you breaking the power of secrecy and shame in your life, you are also taking back the life God intended you to have and restoring your voice! No longer do you have to be bound by secrecy. This is about restoring your Soul Garden, and as you exercise your voice, with each word and each step, you find the healing for which you have prayed.

A MOMENT OF REFLECTION

Before we move on, write down the names of people you could go to as you break the power of secrecy. This list can include a counselor, friend, pastor, or sister, to name a few. Take the time to stop and ask yourself and God whom that could be.

_____

_____

_____

If you don't have someone you feel comfortable sharing with, then you may want to consider finding a counselor. The importance of breaking the power of secrecy is vital to moving forward and finding healing for your Soul Garden.

RECOGNIZING SHAME FOR WHAT IT IS AND WHAT IT IS NOT

Shame has an ability to twist and change our thoughts and perceptions into something they weren't created to be. Let me share two examples of individuals who experienced shame that appeared to be something that it wasn't. The first individual I will call Joey. Shame caused Joey to fear himself and his opinions. Instead of being who he was created to be, he tried to do what he thought others wanted him to do. He was enmeshed with his parents, and his identity came from his parents, not from God. Joey was crippled in making everyday decisions for himself and looked to his parents for help. The only times Joey acted out to stand up for himself was out of anger, and he was immediately reprimanded by his parents. This caused him to back into his shell and hide again and again. Shame wrapped itself into the foundation of who Joey was, and he was unable to live with the joy and freedom he was created to have.

Shame told Joey he should be embarrassed for who he really was, and others would not love and accept him if he revealed his real self to them. He did everything he could to live the way others wanted, but he lost the voice and expression of life that God had placed within him. Over time, as Joey expressed his real thoughts, opinions, and beliefs, he began to feel comfortable with himself. Through therapy, Joey learned to understand his feelings: to not fear them and to express his wants and needs in a healthy manner. He learned that it was okay to disagree with others, and that his family would still love him when he expressed his feelings and thoughts.

Finally, Joey learned the difference between "clear water thinking" (healthy processing) and "dirty water thinking" (unhealthy processing). This equipped Joey to recognize the thoughts and perceptions that shame had distorted and to make the needed adjustments in his thinking process.

The second individual is Lisa. Shame led her to believe that the abuse she experienced as a child was her fault. She blamed herself for her family being split up. Shame led Lisa to believe that as a small child she could control what adults did and therefore, she was to blame. This thinking so entwined itself into Lisa's core beliefs that it was choking the life out of her just like the vines that wrap themselves around trees and plants.

This is a common belief for those who experienced sexual abuse as a child. They believed they could have controlled or changed the situation instead of seeing that they truly had no control over the situation and abuse. It wasn't their fault. This is about recognizing what you have control over and what you don't. Lisa needed to understand that the abuse was not her fault, and this may apply to many of you reading this right now. Lisa was in the process of understanding that she was a child and she physically, alone, could not have stood up to her offender. Lisa did eventually tell what happened, and she was taken into foster care. Shame told her she should have just kept quiet, and then her family could still be together but she did the right thing and spoke up about the abuse. She wasn't to blame, and the one thing as a child she could do was tell, and she did. Recognizing shame for what it is and what it is not helped Lisa understand and accept that.

SPEAKING GOD'S WORD IN YOUR LIFE

> To create new pathways, we need to look to the Word of God and fill our thinking processes with what it says, not what our past experiences say.

Imagine a bike moving back and forth in the same pattern on a dirt road. In time, the bike will make a clear pathway or groove. The groove shows that this path has been taken again and again. When the bike is going on that road, it will naturally gravitate to this groove, this pathway. In our thinking processes, we have experiences that tell us how to handle situations based on past experiences. These create grooves in our thinking, so when something happens, we automatically respond as we have in similar past situations.

To change our thinking processes and to respond in healthy ways, we need to create new grooves. We need to bump the bike out of the groove onto the other part of the road to create new pathways. Over time, the bike will no longer gravitate to the old pathway but go to the new pathway. To create new pathways, we need to look to the Word of God and fill our thinking processes with what it says, not what our past experiences say. Memorizing Scripture helps break the power of shame in our lives and creates new grooves in our thinking processes.

PRAYER

I cannot express strongly enough the importance of prayer in the process of changing one's thinking. I believe with all my heart that prayer has been a powerful key to changing my thinking and breaking the power of shame in my own life. Through the inspiration of Liberty Savard's book, *Shattering Your Strongholds,* I began to pray the way she recommended, and my life truly changed.[9] I prayed that God would bind my mind to the mind of Christ and that His thoughts would become my thoughts. I prayed daily for God to shatter those wrong patterns of thinking—those wrong grooves, those wrong ways of processing situations—and asked Him to replace them with His truth of who I am in Christ. I prayed this daily and know that it was key to the work God did in breaking the power of shame in my life and changing my core beliefs about myself.

I'm no different from you. Our stories and experiences are different, but the power of God is the same for you and me. This takes patience, diligence, and a fighting spirit. This is when we go to war for ourselves through prayer and believe that God is answering our prayers. It's not something that falls on us suddenly and things completely change overnight. It's a process, much like the process of working in our gardens, that takes time, but the benefits of restoration are worth the hard work and patience.

Weeds of Fear, Anxiety, and Control

This year, as I was working in my garden, I found a new plant growing I had never seen before. I immediately thought it was some sort of fungus and quickly cleaned it out of my flowerbed. Surprisingly though, it has shown up again and again, which caused me to do some research on this plant. I found that it was a type of moss called liverwort. What's interesting about this weed is that it has a male and female component to it, and that is how it reproduces. It is normally found in damp soil, and most nurseries consider it a nuisance. However, many have found positive aspects and purposely plant it in their garden for medicinal reasons. For the purposes of this book, we will look at this plant and its negative aspects.

As previously stated, this plant is normally found in damp soil. It is a type of ground cover plant with a leathery and sponge-like leaf. It can stop all nourishment from going through it. So, much like a raincoat that protects us from getting wet, this plant blocks the water from getting through and bringing nourishment to other plants in your garden. It also can block fertilizer from going to the plants. This means the plant blocks all nourishment and the source of life, eventually causing other plants to starve to death.

Management is important with this plant, for without it, the plant will take over and multiply quickly. It also becomes the home for fungus gnats, which can damage roots and spread disease to the plants you want in your garden. What this shows us is that this plant has the potential of having a domino effect in your garden. One thing leads to another and so on and so on.

How do we rid our gardens of this weed? There are many recommendations for different types of chemicals, but if it is surrounding plants that you value and don't want to lose, herbicides are not the best approach. Some surface mulches have been found to be helpful in alleviating this weed, such as hazelnut shells, oyster shells, and filter fabric weed barriers, but these are not welcome by all in their gardens. The combination that works best is an herbicide with reduced watering and fertilizer. This cuts the nourishment from the weed and kills it at the same time. Sometimes plants may need to be moved temporarily to protect them if they are unable to survive the reduced watering. The final important component to eliminating this plant from your garden is sunlight. The sun dries up the soil and naturally kills this plant from your garden.[10] This is an important component to remember as we continue with this chapter.

FEAR-LED THOUGHTS

Fear. Every individual has experienced fear in a variety of forms. God made our bodies to have the fight or flight mode that is associated with fear and anxiety. This aspect serves as a monitor within our brains to release adrenaline when needed to give our bodies the ability to fight or flee from a dangerous situation.

Fear can dominate one's life. Fear is crippling, it can spread, and an individual who is consumed with fear can live a very limited life. Fear says to an individual:

- You're in danger.
- No one is here to help you.
- Save yourself.
- They won't like you if you do what you really want.

We have thoughts of fear that include:

- Fear of rejection
- Fear of what others will think
- Fear of being out of control or loss of control
- Fear of heights
- Fear of driving

In today's society, we are bombarded with fear. On any given day, you can watch the news and be reminded of all that is out there to fear. In the US, since 9/11, we fear terrorist attacks. In the current situation in our country, we fear a financial crisis having a domino effect causing individuals to lose their homes, their jobs, and their bank savings.

We need to understand what fear is and the power that it potentially has in our lives. Remember first that God created the fight or flight mode in our brains for our protection. However, there are times when Satan will counterfeit or distort what God created, and instead of protecting us, we are harmed or destroyed. Fear is an example of this. If the environment continually tells us that we need to be fearful, that our lives are in danger, then fear has become a stronghold in our lives. Fear then has the potential to cripple us. This is the tactic Satan uses to bind us and stop us from fulfilling the full potential of who and what God created us to be.

If you are reading this book, it's more than likely you experienced abuse sometime in your life. For some, it was continual, and for others, it was over a shorter timeframe. Regardless, the way future situations are processed for you can be miscalculated based on faulty thinking. Fear is triggered and read incorrectly within your mind, and that affects how you process information. Situations that are not dangerous or potentially harmful can be perceived incorrectly within your thought process and believed to be dangerous or certainly harmful.

UNDERSTANDING THE BRAIN

Timothy Jennings, MD, describes this process in his video, *Healing the Mind*.[11] He explains that the amygdala, located in the limbic system of the brain, acts like a fire alarm. It goes off when information is processed as a danger to the individual, just like a fire alarm that is pulled when it's believed that there is a fire in a building. The hypothalamus is like the 911 operator who calls for emergency responders to react to the alarm. The emergency responders are the adrenaline and the stress hormones that are released to give the individual the ability to respond to the danger, providing the needed energy for fight or flight. The fire chief, the hippocampus, is there to evaluate and assess the situation and communicate with the 911 operator, the hypothalamus, whether more emergency responders need to be sent out or whether it is a false alarm. The prefrontal cortex is the part of the brain where decisions are made, where we reason, deal with information in mature and healthy ways, and then make decisions based on what we have processed on how to handle the perceived danger.

For an individual who has experienced abuse or trauma, the amygdala is continually shooting off danger signals to the other parts of the brain, and over time, the fire chief, the hippocampus, can become damaged and not do its job correctly. Also, the prefrontal cortex can be underdeveloped as the amygdala is overdeveloped. This means the fire alarm is continually going off that you are in danger or should be afraid, and the part of the brain that helps individuals reason and make decisions is unable to do so.

As a result, someone who has experienced trauma or abuse can have difficulty later in life correctly perceiving situations or experiences. Fear becomes the first response for these individuals, and their lives become fear-led, not spirit-led. Fear has become the stronghold or strong tower that they run to.

SAFETY AND SECURITY

Fear, anxiety, and control have become the strongholds that we run to in all situations in our lives. A stronghold or strong tower is where one runs for safety and protection when there is a perceived danger. When something happens in your life, what is your reaction? Do you run to fear, anxiety, or control? Are these your first responses? Or do you run to God? Is a prayer the first thing on your lips? Strongholds, depending on their source, aren't always healthy or safe for us, but nevertheless we still run to them; it's all we know to do.

Fear, anxiety, and control are symptoms of something greater taking place. They are a result of the abuse, and they are connected to your abuse experience.

Safety and security are a vital part of the foundation in our developmental stages for every individual to have a healthy life. When this has been disrupted, for some over and over again, every reaction is an extension of the unmet need for safety and security. For us to move on in our developmental stages, our cup needs to be filled to overflowing, to have that need met, so that we can move forward to the next stage.

> As you learn to understand that these reactions are a symptom of an unmet need, then you can disarm them and the power they have in your life.

If it's not overflowing in us, if we haven't had our needs of safety and security met, we respond by trying to meet that need ourselves. We do this through the fruits of the unmet need of safety and security, which are fear, anxiety, and control.

What are your greatest fears? What triggers your anxiety and a need to always be in control? What happened in your life that drives you to react in fear, anxiety, or control? As you learn to understand that these reactions are a symptom of an unmet need, then you can disarm them and the power they have in your life.

FEAR

To better understand fear, anxiety, and control in relation to restoring our Soul Gardens, we need to define what fear is because anxiety and control stem from fear. In the *Merriam-Webster Dictionary*, fear is defined as:

1. *archaic*: FRIGHTEN
2. *archaic*: to feel fear in (oneself)
3. to have a reverential awe of <*fear* God>
4. to be afraid of: expect with alarm <*fear* the worst>
5. to be afraid or apprehensive <*feared* for their lives> [12]

Another very common definition of fear that I often use is:

False
Evidence
Appearing
Real

There is so much to be said about fear, and there are a great many books out there that focus on fear and anxiety. For the purposes of this book, our focus is on the weeds of fear, anxiety, and control that come forth in one's life after abuse. Fear affects us spiritually and emotionally, and the effects this has on our souls (mind, will, and emotions) is what we will discuss further.

> Fear blocks all truth, trust, and faith from moving in and through the soul.

Fear, or feelings of fear, can be confusing and distort the reality of what we see, understand, and perceive. These feelings can lead to unhealthy or unreasonable choices because our decisions are based on a feeling of fear, not necessarily on the truth. Fear stops all nourishment from coming into the soul of a person just like liverwort blocks nourishment to the plants around it. Fear blocks all truth, trust, and faith from moving in and through the soul. The soul begins to starve from lack of nourishment of truth because fear has taken over.

Remember, if fear is false evidence appearing real, then our minds, our thought processes, can lead us astray when it comes to this feeling. When our thoughts are fear-based, then our imaginations are fed unhealthy food. This leads to distorted, unrealistic, and overwhelming thoughts or images that have the potential to cripple an individual emotionally.

Fear grows if we feed it. It overtakes one's life and over time, one's life can become more and more limited. Just as liverwort is a carrier of disease, fear spreads like an epidemic if left unchecked. Disease can be spread not only throughout the body, but throughout the soul as well.

In *Overcoming Fear, Worry, and Anxiety* by Elyse Fitzpatrick we read, "Like all of our emotions, fear is experienced both in our mind and in our body, causing intense physical responses. Physically, fear is a felt reaction to perceived danger."[13] Please understand this, fear is experienced both in our minds and our bodies, and it is based on our perceived thoughts of danger. Often, what we perceive as a fearful situation really isn't, but because our imaginations and perceptions tell us something, we believe it to be true.

Fear is about our perceptions, perceptions that are based on our memories of previous experiences, not on the current truth in any given situation. We need to understand this concept right here to break the hold that fear has on us.

Reginald Klimionok tells us in *Overcoming the Giants in Your Land* that, "Fear has been called man's deadliest enemy. Fears—unfounded and unreasonable, tormenting and persistent—can destroy our peace and happiness. Indeed, fear can destroy the total person—body, soul and spirit."[14]

In *Tame Your Fears* by Carol Kent, we find a quote from David Neff: "Fear was designed by God to give our bodies the sudden bursts of strength and speed we need in emergencies. But when fear becomes a permanent condition, it can paralyze the spirit, keeping us from taking the risks of generosity, love, and vulnerability that characterize citizens of God's kingdom."[15]

> However, fear reproduces fear. The more you focus on your fears, the more fears you have.

We need to understand the potential power that fear has in our lives and the destruction that it does to our bodies, souls, and spirits if we allow it to grow and overtake us. Although it may not feel as if you have a choice in regard to fear, in reality, we all do. However, fear reproduces fear. The more you focus on your fears, the more fears you have. Just as liverwort can reproduce itself, fear reproduces more fear. If allowed, fear will grow to the point where your life is limited, smaller, and you have become bound up and fearful to live your life with freedom and peace the way God intends.

ANXIETY

Reneau Z. Peurifoy tells us in *Overcoming Anxiety*, "Anxiety is a normal part of life. It is a 'messenger' that indicates the presence of a problem or issue that needs to be resolved. The more intense the anxiety, the more important the issue. People with severe anxiety often have important life issues they are not dealing with effectively."[16]

Abuse and the trauma of abuse are important issues that oftentimes individuals try to sweep under the rug, and they are afraid, intimidated, or unable to work through them. However, this can result in anxiety that shows up in different areas of one's life. Anxiety can take on many forms in an individual. In the *Diagnostic and Statistical Manual of Mental Disorders,* Fourth Edition, Text Revision (DSM-IV-Tr), we find this can include panic attacks with periods of intense fear or discomfort without the presence of real danger; agoraphobia, the fear of fear, which leads to a pervasive avoidance of multiple situations; panic disorder, which is the reoccurring presence of panic attacks on an ongoing basis; specific phobias that are a persistent fear of objects or situations such as animals, heights, elevators, and enclosed places; social phobias; obsessive-compulsive disorder; post-traumatic stress disorder; and generalized anxiety disorder, to name a few.[17]

The key to understanding anxiety is knowing there is a *perception* that the individual is threatened by something or someone uncontrollable by them or unavoidable to them. Oftentimes, the anxiety occurs without an identifiable trigger. However, remember that the anxiety is reminding us there are issues in the individual's life that have not been dealt with. These issues have been suppressed. It's as if they have been put behind a closed door that has been barricaded and locked, but in reality, the anxiety is the symptom of unresolved issues hidden away behind that closed door.

I wonder how many of you are struggling with this? Do you recognize any unresolved issues in your life right now? You've picked up this book, so this tells me that you may have experienced abuse and that you desire to work through it. Maybe *desire* isn't the right word. Maybe you realize you need to work through it, but the thought of doing so is scary. Remember, God is here with you right now. You are not alone in this.

I encourage you to find a counselor, pastor, or friend to whom you can confide about these unresolved issues. List some possible names of people you can confide in below:

_____

_____

_____

_____

CONTROL

Control. What do you think of when you read this word? Does control mean security to you? If I'm in control, then I will be okay. We need to understand what control really is and what it is not. Control is a false sense of security, a counterfeit "feeling" of being safe. If I control everything, then I will be safe, my family will be safe, and the right decisions will be made. All of these thoughts emanate from the unmet need for safety and security. Control is about our

> Control is a false sense of security, a counterfeit "feeling" of being safe.

flesh trying to meet this unmet need. Control is about the self. Control tells us we have to be in charge, otherwise, it won't get done; we are the only ones who can do it; we are taking care of those we love, or we know what is best for those we love.

In the book, *Untwisting Twisted Relationships* by William Backus and Candace Backus, we read, "If you are a controller, you most likely have certain traits in common with other controlling people. For instance, the way you feel deep inside. No matter how smooth or polished or rough and bossy you may appear on the surface, deep within lies a lump of anxiety. Controlling people not only want their way, they believe they must control everything in order to avoid discomfort. They control so they won't have to worry."[18]

Control is about trying to deal with anxiety in ourselves and not reaching out, talking, or getting help. It's about keeping the barricaded door locked and trying to deal with the symptoms without dealing with the real issues. The distortion says that it's easier to control our lives and others around us than to deal with the issues inside of us. If I'm not in control, then I am fearful of what may happen.

CHOICES IN THE MIDST OF OBSTACLES

As mentioned earlier, we have a choice as to how we will respond when faced with obstacles. Are we going to be fear-led, or are we going to be faith-led? Responding with a choice takes effort. It doesn't come naturally when you are led by fear. However, change can happen, and there is hope. Let's stop and look at some examples in the Bible of those who faced fears and how they responded.

In Numbers 13, we read about the spies who were sent to scope out the Promised Land to see what the people in that country were like. Twelve spies traveled throughout the land and came back forty days later to give their report. The report from ten of them was fear-based and not faith-based. They spoke of the negatives and the what-ifs that lay in front of them in that land. They could not see past their fears and their perceptions of those fears and situations involved in taking over the land.

The other two spies in the group saw things differently. They viewed it all through the eyes of faith. They weren't consumed with what they couldn't do, but instead, were inspired by what God could do. Those two spies didn't see the giants; they saw God!

The ten spies were limiting the plan, direction, and purpose that God had for them. Their lives and spheres of influence became smaller and smaller. See, it's not about the facts; it's how we interpret them that matters. These ten couldn't see God in this situation, they could only see the obstacles. They allowed the feelings of fear to make their decisions for them. On the other side, the two couldn't get past seeing God, and so the obstacles didn't matter. They knew that "with God all things are possible" (Matt. 19:26 NIV), and He would help them to overcome what lay ahead.

Another lesson in the Bible is about David and Goliath (see 1 Sam. 17). It is an additional example of living a fear-based or faith-based life. For forty days, Goliath taunted the Israelites to cross the battle line and fight him. No man was willing to do so. All the Israelites, the warriors, cowered in fear and allowed his mocking words to haunt them. Not only did Goliath bully these men, but he also insulted and cursed the God of Israel.

David came to the battlefield to bring food to his brothers and their commanders. He heard the degrading words of the giant and he became incensed. David looked around at the Israelites and wondered why no one would confront this huge man. He immediately took a stand against this towering giant and with just five smooth stones, a sling in his hand, and a heart filled with faith and belief that God was with him, David conquered the giant.

For forty days and nights the spies traveled in the Promised Land.

For forty days, Goliath taunted the Israelites.

For forty years, the Israelites wandered in the desert.

For forty days, Jesus was tempted.

In the Bible, forty is a symbol for testing, trials, and probation, and it ends with a victory or a defeat. What are the giants, the tests and trials you are facing or have been facing for forty days, months, or years? These giants take on many forms. They may represent painful memories, abuse, depression, rejection, abandonment, fear, helplessness, feeling responsible, isolation and feeling alone, addictions, guilt, flashbacks, self-injury, and/or eating disorders, to name a few.

> We need to learn to not respond to the feelings of fear, but to face our fears.

What are your giants? What are the fears that have ruled your life with an iron fist? We need to learn to not respond to the feelings of fear, but to face our fears. This is what David did and what the two spies were doing as well. God wants us to be faith-led and spirit-led, not fear-led.

KEYS TO BREAKING THE POWER OF FEAR IN YOUR LIFE

RECOGNIZE YOUR TRIGGERS AND THINKING PROCESS

Beginning to recognize our triggers is the first step to change. All of us have them. Some use phrases like "pushed my buttons" or "poked at a sore spot." Regardless of what we call them, they all come from the same source. Understanding our triggers means we need to first recognize that we have unresolved issues in our lives. For those who have been abused, these triggers are often unconsciously associated with the previous abuse. Remember, in our previous chapter, we talked about wearing our sunglasses of abuse? Well, when we wear them, we react to situations based on our perceptions through those glasses.

In *Overcoming Anxiety*, Reneau Z. Peurifoy describes this process as going through a time tunnel. This time tunnel is a conditioned (learned) response that follows us into our adult lives. She tells us that, "The first step in escaping the time tunnel is to identify specific feelings, thoughts, or behaviors that indicate you are experiencing the present as if it were the past and repeating old patterns."[19]

So what are your triggers? You may not be aware of what they are, but God wants us to discover them so we can defeat their control over us. Remember, triggers are an emotional response to something or someone. You're in a situation, and you start to feel fear or anxiety. What is happening right then? What are your thoughts just before that feeling comes? What is the underlying issue relating to your fear? Our thoughts or perceptions are connected to our feelings of fear, anxiety, or control. Identifying those thoughts in each situation will help in identifying your triggers.

Here are some examples of situations where fear, anxiety, and control come to life within us:

1. Fear of rejection: "I don't want to ask for anything from anyone. I'd rather do it myself. I can't deal with someone telling me no. I'm afraid they really don't like me."
2. Fear of unreasonable danger: Your family wants to go to the top of the Space Needle in Seattle, but the thought of going up there is too scary. You may even make it up to the top, but you refuse to look out and stay in the middle of the room the whole time you are up there.
3. Lack of control: As your children become young adults, they pull away from God and quit going to church. You become more and more anxious at the choices they are making. It becomes overwhelming and the anxiety filters through to your day-to-day life.

PRACTICE

Write an example of when you have experienced excessive fear, anxiety, or control in your life.

What was the situation?

What was happening right then? (Describe in detail.)

What were your thoughts just before that feeling came?

What were you feeling? (List all possible emotions.)

What were your thoughts about the situation, self, others, etc.?

What behaviors did you act out?

What was the underlying issue causing your fear to rise?

CHANGE YOUR SELF-TALK

Once we identify the situation—our feelings associated with that situation and the thoughts we have in regard to it—the next step is to change our thinking. Remember, most often, the thoughts associated with our perceptions of the situation are tainted by our past experiences. To break the power of fear, anxiety, and control in our lives, we need to change our thinking.

Let's use situation 2 mentioned earlier as our example in changing our self-talk. In this example, there is a fear of high places causing the individual to feel they are in danger. To change this thinking, there are a few things they need to do. First, the individual needs to stop the panic process in his or her brain. Remember, the emergency responders in the brain have been sent out to help in this situation. They are releasing adrenaline and hormones to deal with the perceived danger.

Grounding skills are vital to stopping panic in its tracks. Here are some of the grounding skills I recommend: Five, four, three, two, one—name five things you can see, four things you can physically feel, three things you can hear, two things you can taste or have tasted today, and one thing you can smell or have smelled today. Hold an item in your hand and describe the details of what you feel while holding it. Visualize a stop sign. Eat a lemon candy. Pray for God's peace of mind.

Next, we need to replace our faulty thinking with healthy thinking. Examples for this situation include:

- "I'm okay. My feelings are telling me that I'm not okay, but I am not in danger."
- "I am surrounded by glass, and I won't get hurt."
- "This is my fear right now, not the truth."
- "I'm safe."
- "This is a reaction to my adrenaline being released. This feeling will subside as I concentrate on relaxing."
- "These symptoms will lessen over time."

How we talk to ourselves in that moment makes all the difference in the world. If we feed on that fear, focus on that fear, and allow those thoughts of fear to rise and overtake us, then we are living our lives as fear-led. To change our stronghold from fear to God, we need to begin with changing our thoughts and what we tell ourselves in each situation.

FACE YOUR FEARS AND BREAK THEIR POWER

Now that we are learning to recognize our triggers and beginning to change our self-talk, the next step is to face our fears. Remember, we have a built-in fight or flee reaction. I want to challenge each one of you with another option when dealing with fears.

> Facing our fears is what David did. He didn't let the words of the giant sidetrack him. He watched the giant, learned about him, and then took the right approach to slay him.

Some of us are fighters. When we fight and it's about survival, fighting for our lives, we can't see beyond our fears, our anxieties, and our need for control. All we see, think, and feel is related to fighting. Others flee. When the feeling of fear or anxiety comes, we run. We take cover, we shut down, which is often referred to as the freeze reaction. We get away in any way possible.

The key is to face our fears by using an entirely different response to these reactions than before. Our fight or flee modes are reactions to a situation. Facing our fears requires something new of us. It means that we begin the process of change and pray that we become responders to a situation, learning to respond as Christ would, not as reactors with others pulling our puppet strings.

This is about learning to face our fears in a safe place and with safe people. Facing our fears is what David did. He didn't let the words of the giant sidetrack him. He watched the giant, learned about him, and then took the right approach to slay him.

We need to look at our fears, investigate them, and understand them and the power they have in our lives. In this process, we discover how and when they started. It's as if you are putting a magnifying glass to that fear and looking at the details to understand your thought process, beliefs, and feelings.

As you dissect them, much like what is done in a science classroom, you will understand in greater depth what that fear is really about. What is the underlying issue? What are those things you fear the most? Why do you fear them? What does this fear look like? What does it smell or taste like for you? Using your full senses, pick up that fear and look at it from all angles, and then write down what you learned. This breaks the power of the unknown and of the fear.

Just as in the *Wizard of Oz* when Dorothy saw the wizard behind the curtain, we need to lift the curtain that surrounds our fears to find out what makes them mysteriously dangerous to us and see them for what they really are.

TRUSTING GOD

This final key to breaking the power of fear, anxiety, and control in our lives is about making God our stronghold or strong tower. Remember, in the past, we have turned or run to fear, anxiety and/or control as our first reaction in a given situation. Trusting God, building a relationship with Him, and learning to turn to Him are vital in overpowering fear. There are four steps to doing this in our lives. It is important to build this stronghold correctly so that it will stand in future situations.

The first step is to build our foundation. This step involves reading and meditating on God's Word, finding Scriptures related to similar situations in our lives, and learning what God says about them. Find those Scriptures, memorize them, and hold onto them. Make them a part of you and the basis, the foundation, to use in time of need.

The second step in building the stronghold of God in your life is the framing. This represents taking those Scriptures you've been memorizing and using them to pray God's Word over your life. God's Word is powerful, and we need to remember to use the combination of His Word and our tongue to proclaim His truth in our lives. This is a powerful tool He has given us that often goes unused.

The third step in this building is putting the walls up onto the framing. Just as the walls wrap around the framing, we need to remember to wrap every situation in our lives with the name of Jesus. God the Father has given us authority in the name of Jesus. We need to use it for our own lives and those for whom we pray.

The final step for building our stronghold is covering the building with a roof. The roof represents the blood of Jesus. Too often we overlook the authority, healing, and restorative power found in the blood of Jesus. We don't want to talk about it, but it's a powerful tool God gave us through Jesus, His Son. But sadly, it has been set aside by many when we pray. When Jesus died on the cross, He fulfilled the sacrifice once and for all for all sin. However, His death was also for our healing and redemption. In Isaiah we read, "But he was pierced for our transgressions, he was crushed for our iniquities; the punishment that brought us peace was on him, and by his wounds we are healed" (Isa. 53:5 NIV). This Scripture foretold of the coming Messiah, who was Jesus, and His purpose of saving the world and bringing a right relationship with God. In the New Testament, we read, "who Himself bore our sin in His own body on the tree, that we, having died to sins, might live for righteousness—by whose stripes you were healed" (1 Pet. 2:24 NKJV). As we pray, we plead the blood of Jesus over our situations and allow His covering to envelop us. This means that Jesus stands in our place in court to plead our case. Through

53

Jesus—His death upon the cross—we have access to God. When we pray, we are asking God to cover us, to heal us, to redeem us, and to heal us by the blood of Jesus.

We then need to pray for the wrong strongholds in our lives to be torn down; for the wrong perceptions and opinions to be destroyed; and for our wrong beliefs, faulty thinking, and false core beliefs to be exposed and destroyed once and for all. Close the prayer by asking God to come in and replace all those wrong ways with His truth, His Word, and His life in us.

A PERSONAL EXAMPLE

As I've briefly shared already, I have experienced abuse in my own life. I did not go to counseling right away; in fact, it was when I became a young adult and had a child of my own that I decided I needed to get help to work through what I experienced.

Shortly after our daughter was born, my husband and I moved two hours away from our hometown. I needed a new start, and moving seemed to be part of the plan God had for us. However, my husband had a hard time finding work locally for the first year and would stay near his job and come home on weekends. Fear began to overtake my life at this point: fear when I drove, fear of being home alone. Fear had surrounded me and was trying to choke the nourishment out of me.

One of the things I became consumed with was checking the locks on our doors. I would check the front and back doors at least fifty times a day. It didn't matter if I had checked it five minutes before, I had to check it again and again. I knew this fear was out of control in my life, and I began to cry out to God asking for help. I was a new Christian, but I was so desperate for love and change in my life that I was open to whatever God asked of me. At the same time, I was actively involved in our church, our ladies' Bible study, and our ladies' prayer group.

The steps I've mentioned previously are the steps God took me through when breaking the power of fear in my life regarding this issue. I knew the fear of being attacked in my home was great in my life. This was the underlying issue for me: safety and security. I felt that if I checked the doors, I would feel safe. God began to take me step by step through changing my thinking and my self-talk.

He then gave me a specific number of times I was allowed to check the locks. Over time, the number became lower and lower until it was down to locking them just once a day. I'm not saying the feeling of fear never rose up again in my life, but now, I was equipped for how to deal with it.

I learned to recognize my triggers, change my self-talk, face my fears, and trust God in my situations. This lesson went far beyond the lesson of checking the locks on the door. It spilled over into other aspects of my life and relationship with God.

Burning Bush of Anger

Our home is on top of a hill overlooking the valley of our small community in the state of Washington. Surrounded by forests of trees, we have one of the most breathtaking views when a gentle fog lies upon the trees in the early morning. It is amazing. We absolutely cherish our home and the moments of serenity we find up on the hill, tucked away from the busyness of life.

As we scan the beauty around us, in pockets on the hills, in the fields, and in the neighboring properties, we spot a bush with beautiful yellow flowers that bloom in June. In fact, when we first bought our house, we went for a drive above our property, and I cut some of these flowers to put in a vase in our home. I was surprised to hear that this flower I thought was so delicate and refreshing was actually a noxious weed that posed a fire danger to our community. When living in a rural community surrounded by forest, it is not something you want on your property.

This dangerous bush is called Scotch broom. It's originally from Europe and was brought to the US to help with land erosion issues and for ornamental purposes. This bush reproduces at a rapid rate; the flowers produce phenomenal amounts of seeds that quickly generate additional plants. The Scotch broom has the ability to tolerate hot and cold conditions; its seeds can remain viable within the soil for many, many years; it forms in dense pockets that overtake other plant life; it has a long life span; and in a fire, it can quickly enflame.

If left on its own, this bush will quickly take over a piece of property and choke out the life of those plants you want to live. To get rid of this noxious bush, it is important to take an aggressive approach. Digging it out and then revisiting the same areas again and again to make sure no new life pops up is a necessity. Pulling the bush up when it's young is crucial to staying on top of this noxious weed. Diligence, hard work, and being consistent are all required in the process of ridding your property of this burning bush, the Scotch broom.

ANGER

Anger. We all have it. For some, it is more explosive, and for others, the anger is focused inwardly. Regardless of how you express it, anger, in itself, isn't bad. It's what we do with our anger that can get us into trouble. Anger is one of the easiest emotions to express. This doesn't mean it's the healthiest expression at times, but for many individuals, it's much easier to express anger than to deal with the underlying issues.

Do you often find yourself ready to explode at the slightest thing? Do you feel anger and frustration rising when things seem out of your control? Are you quick to get angry with someone when they do something that feels like a personal attack? Do you find that you frequently snap at your loved ones?

There are many reasons why we can get angry. Often we focus on what is taking place on the outside of our world, when in reality the issue of our anger is about those hidden issues with which we have not dealt. In working on the next steps to finding healing for our Soul Gardens, understanding our anger, working through those underlying issues, and learning healthy ways to express anger are vital to accomplishing this phase.

In reality, anger is also more socially acceptable. When someone is angry, everyone waits for the explosion and then goes on. But depression, sadness, and grief are all things that make others uncomfortable and our society does not know how to deal with those.

Anger, much like the Scotch broom is quick to reproduce in dense patches, seeds of anger can lie dormant for years if not dealt with, and can spread like a wildfire in our lives and to others.

FROZEN ANGER AND COMPLICATED GRIEF

Many who have experienced abuse were never given a safe place to express their emotions about what was happening. Some of you weren't allowed to express your feelings, especially at home. For others, maybe your abuse was at the hand of a parent or family member, and you were never given an opportunity to say what you really felt. You were trained to hold in your feelings and not express them. This was part of the abuse: Don't share your feelings; shut down and do what you can to survive. This defense mechanism, shutting down and not expressing your feelings about the abuse, protected you at the time but has now become a coping mechanism for life. The abuse may have happened many, many years ago; however, these coping mechanisms are still in place in your life today. You still shut down and don't express your feelings. Often you cannot to label your true feelings, and you do what you do to survive life every day.

Over time, these feelings have built up and anger has become the only way to deal with it. This is frozen anger. In reality, your anger isn't what is frozen. Your emotions or true feelings have become frozen. They haven't gone away. They are always there, right under the surface, but you've learned how to ignore them, and thus they have become frozen. Do you see the similarities to the Scotch broom? Anger, as stated earlier, then becomes the logical way to express anything and everything that you are feeling. Anger has become the conduit to express your emotions.

We can live for years with this frozen anger. Over time, we think or believe that we are okay, and we don't need to thaw out those frozen emotions. Why bother? It's over. Don't bring up the past; you are over it, right? Well, in reality, we do need to thaw out these emotions if we desire to find complete healing, that healing for our Soul Gardens.

Another aspect of dealing with anger in relation to abuse is similar to what professionals call complicated grief. In the grief process, individuals go through the five stages of grief: denial, anger, bargaining, depression, and acceptance. When an individual becomes stuck at one stage of the grief process, it could be due to complicated grief. At this point, individuals often seek professional help in dealing with the grief process so that they can move on to the next stage and eventually work through their grief.

Complicated grief in relation to trauma and anger is just that: An individual has become stuck at one place and is unable to move on with their life. They have become stunted by frozen anger. Anger has become the dominating emotion in this person's life. Anger now dictates their quality of life. It wasn't planned to be that way, but nonetheless, anger is used in expressing all feelings.

So how do we know if we are hiding behind a wall of anger and have other unaddressed emotions? Do you find yourself:

- throwing things
- withdrawing
- yelling
- blaming others
- being hostile toward your own body
- doing self-harm behavior
- slamming doors
- giving the silent treatment

> Anger . . . then becomes the logical way to express anything and everything that you are feeling. Anger has become the conduit to express your emotions.

- being quick to be offended
- using sarcasm
- shutting down in situations that feel threatening
- giving dirty looks (the evil eye)
- banging things around

These are just a few of the signs that anger has become the coping mechanism when dealing with an issue.

BIBLICAL EXAMPLES

Let's return to Genesis 4:2–16 to read the account of the brothers, Cain and Abel. Cain was a farmer and Abel kept flocks. They both had their own areas of service or work. They worked hard and life was good for them both. The problem arose when it came time to give God an offering. Cain gave God fruit from the ground.

We raised our family in central California for many years, and we were surrounded by fruit and nut trees. The fruit on the ground was not the best fruit—we learned that from personal experience. The best fruit were the ripened ones, ready to be picked off the tree. This took additional work. It involved climbing a ladder, checking the fruit, and picking only ripened ones, the best fruit.

The fruit on the ground was fruit we didn't get to before it fell off the trees. This fruit was damaged in the fall and was often over ripened. This isn't to say you can't eat that fruit because you can. The issue here is that it isn't the best fruit, the first fruit.

Abel brought an offering to God as well. He brought a fat offering of the firstborn of his flock. He didn't keep the best for himself, but instead, gave God an offering right from the get go, from his firstborn, not the second, third, fifth, or so on, but the firstborn. This is significant because Abel was honoring God first, and this is what God requires of us. The result of Abel doing this was God's favor. Abel's sole motive was to honor and bless God, not to take a shortcut or hold back the best for himself.

Cain went the easy route, the least sacrificial route, in giving God the fruit off the ground. It didn't cost him as much. The fruit on the ground, his offering, didn't carry the same value as the first fruits that were picked off the tree. God knew this and so did Cain, but when God corrected him, Cain didn't want to hear the truth. Instead of dealing with the issue, Cain became very angry, got stuck in victim thinking, and blamed Abel that God did not approve of his offering.

Cain may have been embarrassed, ashamed, confused, or sad but he was unwilling or unable to deal with his feelings. Instead, he blamed Abel for his problems, became angry at him, acted out in rage, and killed him.

Maybe Cain never learned to deal with his feelings. Maybe Cain was like some of us. It's easier to get mad and focus on other people, issues, or situations instead of looking at ourselves. Maybe we are more like Cain than we realize? You may be thinking, *Well, I wouldn't murder my brother.* However, in reality, we may not physically murder someone, but our actions and words are just as deadly.

The sad thing about Cain is that even after he was caught, he still wasn't able to face his own wrongdoing. Even when God gave him the consequences for murdering his brother, Cain was still speaking from victim-thinking. Never once did he say, "I'm sorry" or "Please forgive me." Instead, he was worried about someone coming after him and killing him. He was more concerned about his comfort than about taking responsibility for his own actions. He was still thinking as a victim.

A PAUSE MOMENT

Do you find yourself blaming others for your problems? Is it easier to point the finger at someone else instead of looking at yourself? Do you struggle with the underlying feelings and find it much easier to become angry and lash out instead of facing those feelings?

Let's take a moment to stop and pray about this:

Lord, I realize, more than I may want to admit it, that I have Cain tendencies within me. I struggle with my own feelings, and I find it easier to put the blame on others. Lord, I don't know how to stop this cycle. I don't want to be this way anymore. Lord, I need Your help right now. Holy Spirit, show me when I am acting out of anger; please show me before I get to the point of rage. Help me, Lord. I need You desperately to come in and open my eyes to the truth of myself. Lord please create in me a clean heart. In Jesus' name, amen.

Cain is a great example of someone who lived with frozen anger. These individuals don't know how to deal with their emotions, so they act out solely through anger.

Another example found in the Bible is the story of Tamar, King David's daughter, who was raped by her half brother, Amnon. We read about this event in 2 Samuel 13:1–38. This tragic story of trauma is one with which many can identify. Maybe you can relate to this story because it is one of abuse at the hands of a family member. Tamar didn't ask for this; she didn't deserve it. She was hurt, abused, and cast aside with no thought to her well-being. It wasn't her fault.

Amnon came in and ravished and destroyed Tamar's Soul Garden. He even went so far as to throw her aside after the rape. He was filled with hatred toward her, and his actions forever left her life shame-filled. Her life was left in ruins, and there was no hope of restoration. All was lost.

Tamar confided in Absalom, her other brother. She was devastated. Her life was destroyed. The trauma of what she experienced forever changed her. She couldn't see life past what had

The abuse you experienced also has a domino effect on the lives of many. If you, too, are stuck in the anger stage of the process, your anger is affecting your health, your life, your family, your relationships, your job, and everything about you.

happened to her. She was crushed. Absalom became enraged and was consumed with anger towards Amnon.

I've contemplated the conversations that may have taken place between Absalom and Tamar over the two years after the rape, before Absalom took matters in his own hands and had Amnon killed. I think Tamar was as angry and infuriated as Absalom was. I think they fed each other's anger. For two years, all Tamar could think about was what she wished she could do to Amnon. Maybe she secretly planned ways she could take revenge on him and shared those thoughts with Absalom. Police departments were not around in those days for her to file a complaint. Amnon was the son of King David, so that didn't appear to be in her favor, even though she was a daughter of King David.

In looking at this tragic story of Tamar from this perspective, I think she could be an example of someone who had complicated grief. Her grief process was stunted at the anger stage. She couldn't get past it. She had become bitter and enraged. She wasn't able to move on in the grief process; she couldn't rid herself of the memories of the abuse. She was stuck. The wound was too great, and she didn't know how to work through the process to healing. She didn't have the resources, a support system, and teaching to help her understand the stages of healing. She was all alone in this, except for her brother Absalom, who was just as angry as she was, if not more.

Maybe as you read this, your eyes are filling up with tears because you can relate to Tamar; you see yourself in her. Your story may be different, but you have been where she is. You didn't have the help you needed. You were all alone. Maybe you've never told anyone. Or maybe, by the time you did share, it was ten, twenty, or thirty years later.

The tragedy is that this trauma had a domino effect on the lives of many. It didn't just affect Tamar and Amnon, it affected the entire family and then some. The abuse you experienced also has a domino effect on the lives of many. If you, too, are stuck in the anger stage of the process, your anger is affecting your health, your life, your family, your relationships, your job, and everything about you.

I know what it is to carry a secret, to not be able to tell others about it.

I know what it is to carry a secret, to not be able to tell others about it. For years, I never told anyone about the two years I was continually molested and raped. I held it in. Later, when I was fourteen, I was date-raped, held captive, and repeatedly abused throughout the night. I couldn't hold that one in, and I told my mother the next day after I could get away. However, I was stunted in my healing process.

When I became an adult, this stunted healing process followed me. Anger was easy for me to express. It was safe. My self-protection was to shut down, and if I did do or say anything, it was out of anger, not the emotion I was really feeling. Anger meant I didn't have to open up those feelings about the experience. It was much easier to just get angry, to explode, and then to move on, or so I thought. Looking back, I see how much my anger affected myself and my family.

A MOMENT OF REFLECTION

As I'm sitting here writing this, my heart is breaking for you. My eyes are filled with tears, tears of understanding. Please know that you are not alone in this. I may not be there physically with you, but I am there with you in spirit. I am praying for you. My support system of friends is praying for you as well. I know the load you have been carrying is heavy and overwhelming at times, but Jesus is standing right there next to you, waiting to take the pain. He is waiting to help you with your anger and walk with you into your healing.

STEPS TO CHANGE

Anger is a powerful feeling, but it is just that, a feeling. The issue is not that we get angry, but it is what we do with our anger that can get us into trouble. This is the area that needs work: learning to manage our anger and not letting our anger manage us.

For us to move out of the habit of responding to every situation in anger, we need to learn to break down our situations and do the work needed to understand the real issues. Following these steps will help us in the next few chapters as we look at the emotions associated with our abuse.

1. Identify the situation/trigger. In this step, write down the details of a situation when you reacted in anger.

2. Identify your body signs. When you started to feel angry, where in your body did you feel it? Did you tighten your fist or clench your jaw? Did you feel your face getting hot or red? Did you grind your teeth? Did your stomach feel like it was in knots? Did your body feel tense all over? Did the pitch or tone of your voice change? Did you feel a tightness in your chest? Was your heart racing? Were your eyes continually blinking or

squinting? These are warning signs our body gives us when we are getting angry. Write down the warning signs you've experienced.

3. Identify the thoughts and feelings regarding the situation/trigger. Remember, we learned in previous chapters that our thoughts affect our feelings. For us to understand this, we need to identify what our thoughts are in the moment. Write down what your thoughts were regardless of how random they may seem. Write down what your feelings were in this situation.

4. Identify how you reacted to the situation. Write down what you did, what you said, and how you acted. Was this reaction appropriate or inappropriate?

NEW COPING SKILLS

For us to break the cycle of inappropriate responses in regard to anger, we need to learn new ways to respond to situations. Remember, many of us have used anger as the fix-all for everything, and to change, we need to learn how to respond appropriately.

The first step is to calm down and not react to someone else's actions. There are three techniques in regard to this step I would like to talk about. All three of these techniques help stop the process of releasing the adrenaline feeding our anger. These important techniques serve the purpose of getting our focus off being angry and helping us calm down so we can make a rational decision about how to respond. With my clients, I explain it this way: Our brains function like a dam with gates that let water out; the "water" that is let out is actually adrenaline. This adrenaline is what fuels our anger. This is part of the fight or flight mode in all of us. When dealing with a situation where anger has become our automatic response, we first need to shut the gates on the dam so the adrenaline doesn't continue to flow. Each of the techniques below serves that purpose.

- Count. Believe it or not, this really does work. This helps your brain focus on something specific, the numbers, instead of on the issue or situation that just happened. As your brain focuses on something different from what you are feeling, the flow of adrenaline that feeds the anger stops. The key is to count the numbers slowly, picture each number, and give yourself plenty of time to count. If you are really angry, just counting to ten isn't going to work. You may need to count to a higher number. Continue counting until you feel yourself beginning to relax. You can count either forwards or backwards.
- Take deep breaths. This is another technique that can help when used correctly. The idea is to focus on your breathing. Picture the air going in slowly and then out slowly. Now remember, don't breathe fast on this one! The key is slow, even breaths and picturing within your mind the air moving in and out.
- Tighten and relax your muscles. In this exercise, the focus is on tightening your muscles, over exaggerating what you may already be doing, and then focusing on relaxing each muscle. Picture in your mind your muscles tightening and then relaxing. This seems to be the favorite of many of my clients!

Next, change your self-talk. This goes back to a previous chapter when we discussed what we think about a situation or event and how it affects the way we feel about it. What is a thought or statement that you can say to yourself that will help you calm down? "It's not worth it" or "Let it go" are both positive self-talk examples. The key is to find one that works for you.

Finally, learn to make an appropriate response. This last step is important because you need to make decisions ahead of time regarding how you will physically respond to the situation. Sometimes we need to talk it out with the person, and other times we need to ignore it. Another situation may involve walking away so that you can calm down. Remember, we don't need to react right away to every situation. Often we need to allow ourselves the time to calm down so we can respond to, not just react to, the other person.

PART 3

Repairing What's Damaged and Destroyed

We will find that parts of our Soul Gardens have become damaged or destroyed in the process of what we experienced. Remember, the trellises, arbors, statues, fountains, and many treasures that once abounded in our gardens are no more. These items, these things, these places in us are what we are going to discuss in the next few chapters.

Imagine with me that you are standing in front of a beautiful mirror. This mirror is unique and has detail and engraving around the edges. This mirror is beautiful and is something you treasure greatly. Sadly, though, the mirror has become damaged. For some, the mirror has a small crack in it or a long fracture moving down across it; for others, severe damage has caused the mirror to become shattered or fragmented.

These different levels or dimensions represent the degrees of damage that take place in our souls, our Soul Gardens, when we have been abused or experienced trauma or difficulties in our lives. The beautiful thing is that God can and does restore the cracked, shattered, and fragmented parts in our lives. He is the balm of Gilead, the Great Physician, and the healer of our souls. Come, let us go with the Holy Spirit and begin the repairing process of those areas in us that are damaged and destroyed.

Damaged Emotions

Imagine with me a place that has no clear boundaries, no beginning and no ending. This place is dark, so dark you can't distinguish one thing from another. The darkness is like a thick, heavy blanket of emptiness weighing down those who live there. This is a place of disorder and confusion. It is void and without form. This place is a chaotic, sloppy mess and those who live there cannot see clearly and have no understanding of what peaceful life really is; they are confused, upset, angry, sad, hurt, depressed, quick to react, and truly unhappy. This place is where many people live. It's a place where all emotions run into one another, and there is no clarity or hope of peace and rest. If there is joy or happiness, it is only for a short time because everything is mixed together and hurt is right under the surface, ready to explode in anger.

Imagine with me a place that has no clear boundaries, no beginning and no ending.

This is a life of someone who has damaged emotions. They desperately want peace, but they don't know how to find it. Everything is mixed together, all feelings, and though they try, it's too overwhelming to find any hope.

Chaos is defined in the *Merriam-Webster Dictionary* as:

1. Obsolete: chasm, abyss
2. The inherent unpredictability in the behavior of a complex natural system
3. A state of utter confusion.[20]

The *Free Dictionary* defines chaos as:

1. A condition or place of great disorder or confusion.
2. A disorderly mass; a jumble: *The desk was a chaos of papers and unopened letters.*
   The disordered state of unformed matter and infinite space supposed in some cosmogonic
   views to have existed before the ordered universe.[21]

The Hebrew word for chaos is *tohu* (toh-hoo): from an unused root meaning, to lie *waste; a desolation* (of surface), i.e. *desert;* fig. a *worthless* thing; adv. In vain: confusion, empty place, without form, nothing (thing of) naught, vain, vanity, waste, wilderness.[22]

These definitions add to the picture of the place where we began our chapter—a desolate place with great disorder, a jumble, a chasm, or abyss—and is used to describe the world before the existence of order in our universe.

In Genesis, the first book of the Bible, chapter 1, we read the story of creation. Before earth was formed, before light was divided from darkness and the boundaries of water and land were set, before life was spoken into being and seasons in life established, there was utter chaos and confusion. In *The Message* we read, "Earth was a soup of nothingness, a bottomless emptiness, an inky blackness." The *New International Version* reads, "Now the earth was formless and empty, darkness was over the surface of the deep." The *Living Bible* tells us, "The earth was a shapeless, chaotic mass." Wow, that truly describes some of our lives. Those feelings that your life is a bottomless pit of emptiness or a chaotic mass can be overwhelming.

The beautiful thing about this Scripture and Scripture in general, is that there is more. God didn't leave earth without form, void, and in a chaotic mess. This is the hope that we have as well. Even though it seems like all our lives have been out of control, chaotic, and confusing, there is hope that God can bring healing to our Soul Gardens.

So why are we a chaotic mess? How do we stop living a chaotic lifestyle? Understanding our emotions is the key to change. Emotions, we all have them. Emotions can be described as a thermometer of sorts that helps us to understand what we are feeling. Emotions help us to know if we are feeling scared, happy, sad, angry, confused, hurt, excited, to name a few. There are hundreds of different feelings that we can pick from when we are dealing with everyday life.

The question is, do we have control over our emotions, or do our emotions rule us? Every one of us deals with everyday situations that may overwhelm us with emotions or feelings. So often, people don't take responsibility for their actions and blame or use their emotional state for an excuse. I understand that some individuals need medication and counseling to deal with their emotional state; however, for some, damaged emotions are related to the abuse. Many are quick to anger, quick to have emotional outbursts or fits of tears. Rage is right on the surface ready to explode, and tears of hurt and confusion are sitting right there ready to burst forth.

Life is confusing. Our emotions are all bunched together like a rubber band ball, and we aren't able to discern what our true feelings are. Everything is a chaotic mess.

Our emotions serve a great many purposes for us. Just as we discussed in the previous chapter on anger, our emotions or feelings are not bad in themselves. We react with negative behaviors in relation to how we are feeling at the moment. Often, this is our self-protection. We do what we do to protect ourselves. We were taught to do that to survive. Unfortunately, we are often like hamsters on a wheel, going around and around the same issues in our life without any change.

The one thing we need to be aware of, though, is that our feelings can deceive us. My feelings can tell me I'm in danger, that someone is attacking me with their words or actions, or that I've been betrayed. These feelings are based on my perception of what happened. Remember the glasses of abuse we wear? Those glasses distort our perceptions, our abilities to process information correctly because our perceptions have been damaged based on past experiences.

I may feel I've been hurt because my emotions and my ability to process the information of the situation have been damaged. I then react according to my perceived hurt, betrayal, rejection, or whatever feeling I have at that moment.

So in relation to our abuse experiences, just as we learned regarding anger, often we are not taught to understand or we are not given the skills to work through our feelings. The easiest way to deal with our feelings, as we have been taught, is to shut down or to explode in anger. Remember, our emotions can be unpredictable, uncontrollable, and unmanageable when they are damaged.

A PERSONAL EXPERIENCE

I was raised by a single parent. My mom worked hard to support my brother and me. We had a roof over our heads, food to eat, and clothes to wear. We didn't have a lot, but we had just enough to get by. My mom did nearly all of the raising of my brother and me. She didn't get the support and help she needed from my dad. They divorced when I was a baby, and I don't remember him as part of our family. All I do remember is a couple of times a year when we would be whisked off for the weekend to spend time with our dad and his family. This lasted until I was about fifteen years old, but I will get to that later.

My mom was raised in a very strict military family. There are many rules that she changed within her family structure from the strict military life in which she was raised, but one important aspect of growing up did not change: the inability to express feelings. If I became emotional, cried, or was upset, I was sent to my room. The message I was given as a child was that emotions were uncomfortable. If I displayed my emotions, I was sent to my room and was not allowed back with the rest of the family until my emotions were "under control." I wasn't comforted, taught, or equipped in how to deal with a variety of situations that triggered different emotions in me. Instead, I learned how to stuff and avoid my emotions.

I was the perfect mark when I was approached by two older neighborhood kids and the two years of sexual molestation and assault began. Since I was taught to not share what I was really feeling, I kept it all in. I didn't know how to talk about it. I wasn't given a platform to share about my day-to-day life, so why would I share when I was being abused.

The experience of being raped at age fourteen taught me to shut down to a level I had never known before. Shutting down became my means of survival to a much greater degree. The abuse, the aggressiveness, the acts during the rape, were all overwhelming, and I lived in survival mode. But this time I did tell. However, the experience of what happened after I told was too overwhelming for a teen. I didn't have the skills or the understanding to work through my emotions.

After this experience, many pivotal things began to take place in my life. My father, after hearing of the rape, promised he would be there for me. He, of course, was not. Within a year after the incident, my father moved. I didn't hear from him or see him for about fifteen years. My friends, the ones I felt comfortable talking to about the rape, weren't equipped to deal with the emotional mess I was, so they pulled away from me. When charges were placed against the man who raped me, my name was to be kept confidential, but that didn't happen. It became the talk of the town, and many turned against me. These developments taught me to keep quiet, to not share what's really going on because nobody really cared anyway.

Following these setbacks, I began a deep plunge into the world of drugs. I had found the best way to shut down. Do drugs and your life goes numb, or so I thought. All of these—drugs, disappointments, and the lack of skills—taught me that you don't express your feelings. You don't face them; instead, you stuff them in a trunk, put them in a dark room, shut the door, and barricade it so nothing can come out.

This became my way of living for many years. Occasionally, I would try to open that door and peek into the trunk, but I would break down in an emotional mess. I wasn't able to identify why or what those feelings were in the locked trunk, and I didn't have the correct tools to work through them. It was too overwhelming for me. Everything was knotted together like a rubber band ball. I couldn't separate one feeling from another. I was without form, void, and in a place that was surrounded by darkness. There was no hope to be found. I couldn't go on. I needed a Savior to rescue me and heal my Soul Garden. It was in that desperate place at the age of twenty-one when I asked Jesus into my heart, and my life was forever changed for the good. It didn't always feel good, but God came in and began the process of restoring my Soul Garden.

THE GOD OF HOPE

Let us go back to Genesis 1 in the Bible. To this point, we have discussed the void, emptiness, and chaos that earth once was. We discussed this in relation to our own lives and how they, too, can be a chaotic mess. The hope and the beauty of the story of creation is that this was just the beginning. We are given a sign of hope from the get-go when we read on.

What I didn't mention before is that even though the earth was without form, void, and the darkness was vast, the Spirit of God was right there in the midst of it all, hovering over it. The Spirit of God is right there in the middle of our chaos, our darkness, and our emptiness. God is here. His Holy Spirit is moving back and forth over us in our chaos. He's concerned about us; He's patiently waiting for us, and He's sitting with us, and over us, waiting for that moment when life will come forth once again.

The Spirit of God is right there in the middle of our chaos, our darkness, and our emptiness.

Remember, in our Soul Gardens, the place God is restoring, there are many beautiful treasures that have been damaged by the vandals who came into our gardens. In the restoration of our Soul Gardens so far, we have called upon the Master Gardener to come and help with the process of pulling out the weeds and planting God's Word and truth in our garden. Now, we need the Master Carpenter to come in and do repair and restoration work on those damaged and, in some cases, destroyed treasures. The Master Carpenter is right here ready to repair our damaged emotions. All we must do is ask. God is waiting to help, to heal, and to restore those broken and damaged places in our lives. Nothing or no one is beyond repair. No job is too difficult for the Master Carpenter. He is here, hovering over us, waiting for us to ask.

Nothing or no one is beyond repair.

If we were to see what the earth looked like at the beginning, before God spoke, we would probably think, "Give up on that one, God. There's no hope. Can't you see the mess that earth is?" These are similar thoughts we may have of our chaotic mess. It may seem that there is no hope, but the hope is that God is with us in our chaos. He's with us in our mess, and He's not leaving. He's patiently waiting for that right moment for life to come forth, for us to invite Him to heal us, to begin the work in us and to change us. He's here. Can you feel Him? His presence, His power, His life is with us and we are not alone.

The next event changed earth forever. God spoke light into existence and divided the darkness from light. This is the place where the Holy Spirit began to bring order, God's divine order, to the chaotic mess of earth. Here is a valuable truth we need to understand; the Holy Spirit brings order to our chaotic mess. When we allow God into our lives, when we allow Him to speak into our lives and we respond, God will start the process to separate our emotions from one

Here is a valuable truth we need to understand; the Holy Spirit brings order to our chaotic mess.

another and help us with the memories, with our overwhelming feelings, and begin the motion of bringing order to our lives.

Oh, I find so much hope in this! I remember being in that place and God beginning the process of bringing order into my life. One by one, I began to unpack the trunk one emotion at a time and one memory at a time. The Holy Spirit was and still is at work in my life. The Holy Spirit is here to do the same thing for you. The first step we need to do now in this process is pray and give God permission to come in and do the work that we desperately need done in our lives. A prayer:

Lord, I give You permission to come into my life, to bring that divine order I so desperately need. I'm tired of living like this. I need You to begin the process of separating and dividing in my life, just as You did in creation. I give You permission to come into my life and to do this work. Holy Spirit, I need Your help, Your guidance, and Your counsel as I take one memory and one feeling at a time out of the trunk where I hid them away. Help me with this. When fear overwhelms me or anxiety has me stretched beyond what I can bear, Lord, I need Your peace and Your presence to surround me. Lord, Your Word says that we can do all things through Christ who gives us strength. Give us the strength and courage we need for this. In the book of Joshua, You reminded him again and again to be bold and courageous as he went into uncharted land, into the Promised Land. Lord, help us to remember those words and to be bold and courageous ourselves as we go into these memories and face our feelings in this uncharted land in our Soul Gardens. Be with us through this. In Jesus' name, amen.

Now that we have prayed and asked God for His help with this, let's look at how our emotions serve us. The first purpose of our emotions is for arousal or a strong impulse. The smell of perfume, the sight of someone we care about, and the voice of a loved one on the phone can arouse what we are feeling when we encounter these things. This arousal can be toward either positive or negative feelings depending on what the memory is associated with. For some, the smell of something such as shampooed carpet, air freshener, a certain food, or burning wood, for example, can trigger negative emotions.

The trigger can be a conscious or unconscious memory. If it is an unconscious memory, the individual can feel negative emotions but not be aware of why. In young children, memories are not stored in pictures, but in the senses. As an adult, something can negatively trigger our memories through smell, taste, or touch, and we may not be aware of this because it has triggered a memory from our early childhood. If abuse began early in life, these unconscious triggers can be taking place without us being able to connect them to past abuse.

The second purpose of our emotions is to motivate us into action. Fear can motivate me to run, hide, or cry. Other times joy or excitement can motivate me to jump up and down, squeal with excitement, or laugh. The fight or flight mode in all of us is a motivator in dealing with situations that threaten us.

The final purpose for our emotions to focus on is how they are like a GPS or guiding system within us. These feelings, when triggered, lead us into decisions of action—of what to do in a situation. When we see a sunset, our GPS tells us we are enjoying a moment of beauty. A baby's laugh, an eagle soaring in the sky, and waves crashing on the shore all trigger different, but in some cases, similar feelings in us. Our emotions lead us in these situations.

GOD'S DIVINE ORDER

Now we need to begin the process of dividing and separating our feelings in our lives, in our Soul Gardens. This process helps us to identify our feelings. To do this, we need to broaden our vocabulary of feelings. Below are lists of a few positive and negative emotions.

POSITIVE EMOTIONS

pleased	glad	wonderful	elated
excited	content	surprised	proud
satisfied	confident	hopeful	comfortable
calm	relaxed	warm	ecstatic
grateful	joyful	lively	love
pleasure	positive	open	stable
thrilled	expectant	energetic	eager
determined	able	courageous	worthy
great	fascinated	capable	excellent
charmed	beautiful	happy	adequate
noble	peaceful	understanding	inspired
enthusiastic	delighted	creative	agreeable
expressive	humorous	powerful	silly
passionate	compassionate	responsible	important

NEGATIVE EMOTIONS

nervous	frustrated	weak	irritated
tense	annoyed	furious	livid

anxious	enraged	hurt	inadequate
flustered	trapped	tired	scared
insecure	embarrassed	used	jealous
angry	overburdened	disgusted	contempt
cross	flat	insecure	defeated
confused	threatened	despairing	miserable
bored	shocked	terrified	ashamed
apathetic	lonely	discontented	uncomfortable
foolish	aggressive	envious	fearful
stupid	pitiful	moody	frightened
awkward	preoccupied	uneasy	greedy
grieving	guilty	sad	depressed
impatient	belligerent	repressed	resentful
helpless	hatred	broken down	bullied
shut down	isolated	low	hopeless
panicked	paranoid	withdrawn	

These are just a sample of the hundreds of emotions we could have. Now we will begin the process of identifying our own feelings. To start with, we will not focus on the feelings of our abuse but learn how to identify feelings in our own day-to-day lives.

Look back at the list of positive and negative emotions. Thinking about today and during the past week, list three to five emotions you experienced:

1.
2.
3.
4.
5.

Now in thinking about each emotion individually, use the statement below to further discover your feelings. Write one of the emotions you chose after the word *felt*, and then after the word *because*, describe the reason you felt that way. Do this for each emotion you chose.

I felt _____ because_____.

I felt _____ because_____.

I felt _____ because_____.

I felt _____ because_____.

I felt _____ because_____.

This is an exercise that should be done on a daily basis using the list provided, or you can do further research online and compile a more detailed list.

The point behind this exercise is to learn to identify your feelings and become comfortable with that process. As this becomes comfortable and familiar, then and only then do you begin the process of visiting those feelings associated with memories. For some, this process is best done with the help of a counselor.

The next step in this process of healing damaged emotions is finding a creative outlet to express those feelings. Different venues can be used for this process. Some examples are:

- writing poetry
- songwriting
- drawing
- abstract painting
- collages to describe each feeling
- journaling
- photography
- sculpting
- pottery
- gardening
- writing
- playing an instrument

This is really up to the individual to find what outlet to begin the process of expressing their feelings and allowing those things that have been hidden to come out in a safe way.

The key to healing our damaged emotions is learning to understand our emotions, not just ignoring them; learning to identify our emotions in relation to our day-to-day lives

> The key to healing our damaged emotions is learning to understand our emotions, not just ignoring them; learning to identify our emotions in relation to our day-to-day lives and eventually to our trauma experiences; and learning to express those emotions in healing and productive manners.

and eventually to our trauma experiences; and learning to express those emotions in healing and productive manners. This will strengthen us as we go into the steps of dealing with memories and feelings. Keep following the process you have learned in this chapter regarding discovering your feelings; be patient with yourself and allow God to heal your damaged emotions one day at a time.

BEING GOD-LED VERSUS EMOTION-DRIVEN

Another aspect of damaged emotions we need to look at as we learn to separate our emotions and understand them, is learning to be God-led in difficulties and day-to-day situations versus being emotion-driven or reactive. Earlier, when we defined chaos, one of the words used in the Strong's definition was wilderness.

Wilderness is used to describe chaos. How often do we all feel like we live in the wilderness, where there seems to be no end to the trials, where there is no hope? Remember in the Old Testament when the Israelites found freedom from slavery then lived in the wilderness for forty years? For forty years, they were emotion-driven. They reacted to each obstacle or difficulty based on their feelings and not on God's promises.

The Israelites were emotion-driven, and their emotions were in charge despite all that God had done for them. An example, which we discussed in earlier chapters, showed the two sides of this in Numbers 13 and 14 when spies were sent to Canaan to check out the land God had promised to give the Israelites. Joshua and Caleb were the only two who came back from spying out the land who were still God-led. All the others were swayed by fear, intimidation, and the circumstances. They were emotion-driven, unable to see how God could give them victory if they went into the Promised Land.

How often do we feel this way? In our situations, difficulties in our lives, or obstacles we are facing, we focus on the circumstances instead of trusting God to do what He said He would do for us. For many of us, trust is a big aspect of this. We haven't been able to trust because of the hurt we've experienced, and now God wants us to trust Him? Just how do we do that?

The next step in trusting God is learning to not let our emotions drive us to wrong reactions. Our emotions are one of the greatest deceivers in our lives. Just as the spies had two sides to what they saw—one saw giants that would overtake them, the other saw the blessings God had for them in this new land—there are two sides to all our situations.

Ten of the spies had on their abuse sunglasses. They viewed the situation through their sunglasses of hurt and abuse from years of being slaves in Egypt. They could not get past their perceptions and experiences of past hurt. They were unable to see hope in the new opportunities and blessings God had for them. How many of us are just like this? If we were together in a room many, if not most, of our hands would be up in the air.

Learning to move beyond being emotion-driven means we learn to recognize that often our perceptions, our thought processes, trigger our emotions in the wrong way, and then we are deceived. The Israelites had experienced abuse and neglect for years at the hands of the Egyptians and thus, their perceptions were distorted by their past experiences. Our perceptions can be distorted by our past experiences as well. This is fuel to the fire for our emotions to deceive us.

ELIJAH: A GREAT MAN OF GOD

At this point, some may be feeling discouraged, thinking that you may never grasp all this teaching. Others may be thinking, "God, how can I do great things for you if I'm emotion-driven?" Remember, we are all a work in progress, and no one has arrived to a completed level of work, no one but Christ because He is God. However, the Master Carpenter is here to repair and restore that which has become broken, shattered, and destroyed in our lives. Nothing and no one is beyond repair.

Elijah was an example of a great man of God who, at times, was emotion-driven not God-led. In 1 Kings 18 and 19, we read that Elijah took on the prophets of Baal at Mount Carmel. God used Elijah to show His people that, indeed, He was the only true God and Baal was a false god who could not do anything for his people. This event was one of the greatest moments in Elijah's life, and God used him greatly to expose evil, to destroy the false prophets, and to demonstrate His great power.

However, after this great victory, Elijah was driven by fear and his emotions into the wilderness. He was fearful for his life at the hand of Jezebel who was married to King Ahab. Elijah could not see past her words of destruction, and he was driven to the wilderness by fear and anxiety. As Elijah's emotional state was in chaos—the wilderness—other emotions were triggered as well. Elijah didn't stop at fear and anxiety. Next, he became despondent and suicidal. He prayed and asked God to let him die. Can you imagine? Hours before he had had his greatest victory and now here he was, emotion-driven and wanting to die.

God ministered to him in that place, right where he was, in the middle of the wilderness, in his chaos, just as God ministers to us amid our own chaos. We need to remember that God is with us in the midst of our difficulties, our confusion, and our emotion-driven state. God sent an angel to nourish Elijah: He ate and drank, he slept, and then the angel came back again to feed him and give him instruction.

In the midst of our chaos, our wilderness, God is here to do the same for us. We may or may not have an angel sent to us; it could be a friend, something we read in God's Word, a sermon preached on Sunday morning, or a song played on the radio. Regardless of what it looks like, God sends us the nourishment we need to get through the season in the wilderness.

Now, Elijah did have a choice: to get out of the wilderness or to go further in. Sometimes, we can't see how to get out of the wilderness, so we go in further and deeper, just as Elijah did.

His depressive state drove him into the bowels of the wilderness in the middle of chaos. The wilderness called to him. Depression called to him. Elijah went deeper into his depression. Often, this is our own story. One thing is triggered; we are driven by those emotions, and then other emotions are triggered, which drive us into the depths of our own wilderness state of hopelessness.

For forty days and nights, Elijah was driven by his emotions. Forty days and nights represent our time of testing. Elijah was running from something. What are you running from? What are those situations you are having difficulty facing? Remember when we discussed fear in an earlier chapter? Learning to face those things that we fear the most, one by one, is part of learning to be God-led and not emotion-driven. How do we do that? How do we learn to face those things that we fear the most? Our emotions can be scary and can represent such uncertainty and memories we may not want to consider.

Learning to recognize our triggers is vital to changing how we respond in situations. The next step in learning to identify our feelings and divide and separate our emotions from one another is understanding how each emotion affects us. Earlier, we identified positive and negative emotions. Now we are going to divide our emotions into their primary emotion category. I work with clients of all ages to help them learn this process. The process helps us understand our emotions and with what they are associated.

HAPPY	SAD
excited	hopeless
thrilled	humiliated
alive	empty
joyful	despair
creative	shame
grateful	alone
enthusiastic	cold
hopeful	bored
content	guilty
cheerful	stupid
connected	depressed
jovial	worthless

lighthearted	inferior
vivacious	tired
	regret

ANGRY	FREE
furious	loved
bitter	valued
devastated	appreciated
frustrated	open
hurt	worthwhile
resentful	respected
betrayed	friendly
cheated	complete
offended	sincere
irritated	important
controlled	forgiven
sarcastic	empowered
jealous	
disgusted	
FEAR	SAFE
trapped	trusting
paralyzed	relaxed
overwhelmed	secure
threatened	calm
crazy	encouraged
helpless	understood

bewildered	confident
abandoned	cozy
shocked	protected
embarrassed	quiet
numb	warm
rejected	accepted
worried	
weak	
defensive	
vulnerable	
inadequate	
foolish	
confused	
scared	

When we list emotions under these categories, it brings an understanding to the root trigger we may not have been aware of before. An example of this is feeling bored; bored is under the primary emotion of sadness. Or how about feeling abandoned? Abandoned is under the primary emotion of fear. By breaking this apart, it provides a better understanding of what is taking place at the root level.

The next step is learning to recognize our feelings and how our bodies react to them. As we put our feelings under a magnifying glass, we can better understand them and recognize when they are being triggered within us.

EXERCISE

1. Identify one feeling: _____

2. Identify where in your body you feel this emotion. What is happening in your face, in your arms and hands, in your legs, in your stomach? Think about all parts of your body and write down what is happening within your body.

3. What changes do you notice in your voice and in your speech?

4. What are your thoughts when you have this feeling? What are you telling yourself?

5. What changes can you make in your thinking process or your self-talk when this feeling is triggered? What needs to change?

6. How do you act when you have this feeling?

7. What changes can you make in your reactions when this feeling is triggered? Which reactions are healthy and unhealthy? Appropriate or inappropriate?

We need to remember that often what we tell ourselves isn't the truth; it's based on our perceptions or opinions and not based on the truth. Our perceptions are shaped by our core belief systems of ourselves and others. These are based on our experiences and whether our needs were met as a child. When we have not been given a place to express our emotions in a healthy manner, we need to learn how to do that. Taking these steps to understand our feelings and how

> We need to remember that often what we tell ourselves isn't the truth; it's based on our perceptions or opinions and not based on the truth.

they affect our body and our self-talk and how we react are all part of the process to change from being emotion-driven to God-led.

Finally, the last exercise we will do is a creative art piece. Often, we may struggle with writing down what we are feeling, but when we use art forms, we can express feelings that we couldn't otherwise. Take a piece of blank paper and using paints, chalk, pastels, watercolors, colored pencils, crayons, or pens, create an art piece that represents your heart, your soul. Within that heart will be a variety of colors. Each color represents a feeling. Go through the lists from earlier in the chapter and identify which feelings you believe are in your heart. Some colors may be used more than others, as some emotions or feelings are stronger or have a larger place in us than others. Each color represents a specific emotion, so be creative in the process.

You can do a second art piece that represents the feelings you would like in your heart. This can be something you keep as a reminder, something to encourage you as you are doing the work needed to get to that place. Remember, it is possible because, "all things are possible with God" (Matt. 19:26 NIV). If He can do it in my life, I know, without a shadow of a doubt, He can do it in your life as well.

A MOMENT TO REFLECT

Stop and take the time to reflect on the two art pieces you created. What do they represent to you? What changes would you like to see? Ask God what changes He would like to do in you.

A PRAYER

Lord, thank You for each person who has read this chapter. I know, Lord, that learning to understand our feelings can be uncomfortable. Give each person the strength and courage to do the work that is necessary. Lord, we want to be healthy; we want to grow and become the fullness of what and who You created us to be. Thank You for giving us strength and the ability to walk through this process. Help us, Lord, to understand and identify our feelings. Thank You that we are not alone, and You are with us in the midst of our chaos, our wilderness place. Help us through this process, walk with us out of the chaos, and may we see ourselves the way You see us. In Jesus' name, amen.

Damaged-Goods Thinking

This week, my thoughts have been about the damaged-goods thinking process that many of us experience. Damaged. What does that mean? Damaged denotes that something has impaired value, or its usefulness has changed or, even more harsh, its normal function has been severely affected. When difficult things like trauma or abuse come, this is what can happen. Abuse takes on many forms; one form in particular is that someone who has been abused can have their thinking about themselves damaged.

As a teenager, I recall feeling the need to protect my friends from what I experienced, and in certain situations, I would sacrifice myself to protect them. I was already damaged from the sexual abuse. I wanted to protect them from situations that felt dangerous to me. One time, a friend and I were walking down a secluded road, and there was a very large man walking toward us. Immediately, I felt uncertain about this man and could feel a chill up my spine as he came closer and closer to us. In my hometown, there were many homeless people, hippies, and individuals who wandered the streets, so seeing him wasn't abnormal, but there was something about this man that made me very uncomfortable. The road was a secluded one with one side filled with trees and a creek, and the other side was a hill. There were no houses, no people, no one to call for help near us. We stopped for a moment to decide what to do. We finally agreed to keep walking toward him, but that I would stand on the outside, near him, so that I could protect her. I remember telling her, "I've already been damaged, I don't want that to happen to you, too."

We headed down the road. I was apprehensive as we walked closer and closer, but we didn't turn back. The moment we walked past him, I was shaking inside, but true shock hit me when he grabbed me, and I screamed, "*Run*" to my friend. We got away and called the police. Of course, the man was never found, but my thoughts were not so much of my safety, but of my friend's.

My self-image was that I was already damaged. I was not just a mirror with a chip; I was a mirror that had been fractured or better yet, shattered. There was no hope for me, at least that's what I felt, but I could protect my friend. I was broken already, damaged, of no use any more. I thought I was beyond repair.

I know that I'm not alone in feeling this way. This thinking seems to be universal with those who have experienced abuse, especially during childhood.

SHATTERED GLASS: OUR SHATTERED IMAGE OF SELF

> However, this amazing man named Jesus came into my life and began to show me that I was not beyond repair as I had thought.

Shattered glass. What do you think when you hear those words? What images come to your mind? I see a treasured glass statue or maybe a mirror that someone has dropped, and it has shattered into millions of little pieces. Everywhere I look, I can see pieces of the glass. All hope of that precious treasure being what it once was is now gone. With hope gone, only devastation is left in its place. Boy, that's how I felt when I was younger. I felt shattered, destroyed, and completely broken beyond repair. However, this amazing man named Jesus came into my life and began to show me that I was not beyond repair as I had thought. He showed me that His love and healing came day by day as I grew deeper in my relationship with Him. As I sought out help from godly people who could walk me through the process of restoration, I slowly began the journey of healing and restoration for my Soul Garden.

Shattered. What does this word mean? I've shared my thoughts on this word, but I began to ask myself what the official definition is. The word *shatter* is defined in the *Free Dictionary* online as: "To cause to break or burst suddenly into pieces, as with a violent blow; to damage seriously; disable; to cause the destruction or ruin of; destroy; to break into pieces; smash or burst."[23]

As I read this definition, my eyes began to well up with tears. My heart breaks because so many of us fit this definition. When the abuse began in my life, it felt like a violent blow, you know, the kind that takes your breath away; you want to gasp for air, but you can't. It's the type of violent blow that's life changing, damaging, shattering, and gives you the feeling deep inside that nothing would ever be the same again. Joy was gone; pain was in its place. Hope of a future was gone, and a lack of zeal had taken its place. Laughter was replaced by tears, freedom became bondage, and value was taken over by the concept that I no longer had worth; I was now broken and no good to anyone.

Does this sound familiar to anyone? Yeah, I thought so. I know that I am not the only person who has felt this way.

I'M A BAD PERSON, THEREFORE I DESERVE BAD THINGS TO HAPPEN TO ME

Is this a thought you have had about yourself? Are you filled with self-hatred and blame toward yourself? Do you, at times, think you deserved it? I don't know about you, but that became a vital part of my self-talk and my core beliefs, my value as a person. I was bad; therefore, I deserved and expected that bad things would happen to me on a regular basis. I didn't deserve good things. Back then, I would probably disagree with some of these statements; that is called denial. But deep down inside, that was how I felt about myself. I would have told you that a good life just wasn't in the cards for me.

My self-image was changed. I began to think, see, feel, and react through the concept that I was bad, dirty, and worthless. Damaged goods thinking told me that:

I'm . . .

bad	terrible	unpleasant
evil	wicked	marred
inferior	flawed	faulty
defective	naughty	wayward
unhealthy	trouble	damaged
broken	rotten	decayed
useless	meaningless	rubbish
unworthy	no good	ugly
crazy	invisible	stupid
inadequate	dirty	not good enough
unlovable	repulsive	selfish
at fault	to blame	no good
insignificant	empty	valueless

Take a moment to circle the words that describe how you feel or think about yourself today. Put an X next to those words that describe how you felt about yourself in the past.

I'm sure there are other words that can go on this list. The point is, I believed the lies and began to see myself in the way God had not intended. My circumstances defined me, not God. My value and self-worth plummeted deep down into the pit of distortion and despair. This was not what God intended for me, and it's not what God intends for you either.

HURTING AND NEEDY PEOPLE

> My value and self-worth plummeted deep down into the pit of distortion and despair. This was not what God intended for me, and it's not what God intends for you either.

Every single individual in the world is a hurting and needy person. No one can bypass it. To understand this, we must go back to the days of Adam and Eve when they first took a bite of the apple—the bite changed their view of life, of each other, of God, and most importantly, of themselves. It was at this point in history that all mankind became hurting and needy; it changed our view of the world and ourselves.

Hurting and needy people hurt people. It's not always intentional, although at times it is by some. Out of our hurt and pain, we harm others in words, actions, deeds, and through various circumstances. Our victim thinking, offenses, destructive behaviors, chaotic emotions, faulty thinking, opinions, and wrong interpretations of another's motives all lead us to hurting others. It is an unhealthy cycle we follow that leads us to thinking of ourselves only. Now, please hear me when I say this. I'm not making excuses for what was done to you; I'm making a general statement about how we find our value and worth through others. We look to one another to fill those empty places within us. When the relationship between God and mankind was changed through Adam and Eve, our thinking became distorted. Mankind began to look at each other for value instead of to the only true one who can give this to us, God. Our distorted, hurting-and-needy-people thinking tells us that someone else defines whether we are adequate or have any worth, and at times, it defines our purpose.

In comes abuse. The words that are spoken to us, the way we feel about what is happening, all tell us we deserved this, we are to blame, we are dirty, we are bad, and we brought it on ourselves. Have those thoughts gone through your mind? They have mine.

HAGAR: A WOMAN WHO WAS USED AND ABUSED

When we hear the story about Abram (Abraham) and Sarai (Sarah) in Genesis 16, the focus is usually on the choices they made about trusting God for their future. God had spoken to Abram ten years before and promised that he would have children, a legacy that would go on for generations. For ten years, they held on to that promise, but then they became weary in trusting God's timing and decided to take matters into their own hands.

Rarely do we ever hear sermons or teaching on Hagar, the slave girl from Egypt. Abram and Sarai used her to serve their own needs and wants without a thought of Hagar herself. Abram and Sarai where both hurting and needy people who hurt Hagar in the process of trying to get their answer—children—without her consent.

Now, Hagar is mentioned in the Bible and in sermons, but it often seems she is put in a bad light. The Bible states that once Hagar became pregnant, she despised Sarai, and some say that she looked down on her. Let's look at this from a different perspective, from Hagar's perspective, not Abram or Sarai's.

Hagar was a young slave girl. She was a foreigner and her name meant *stranger*. Hagar was used, mistreated, and abused for someone else's purpose. Hagar didn't have a choice. Imagine this young girl who is told to have sex with Abram. She wasn't asked to be a surrogate or if she would even be interested in doing this, she was just told. Abram was eighty-five years old; Hagar was a young slave girl. How scary this must have been for her! She had no choice; she was just used for someone else's purpose and then mistreated later.

What do you think Hagar thought about this? Do you think it was what she wanted? Do you think she put herself in that position? That she deserved it? That she was to blame for all the problems? Do you think Hagar felt unloved, persecuted, defiled, abandoned, used, and invisible? I do. I think she was used, and when she was being treated well for being pregnant, better than she had been before, she was punished for liking it. I'm not saying she's perfect. No one is. But she was used to meet someone else's needs and then blamed and persecuted for how she handled it.

Does this sound familiar? It does to me. I think Hagar's thoughts were much like ours. I'm to blame, I'm dirty, I'm unlovable, I'm bad, I'm . . . You fill in the rest of the words. Then, later on, others don't always agree with how we handled our abuse and often, once again, we are abused through actions and words that others speak about us.

Hagar did have an encounter with God later in the story. It's at that point that she changed. Her value, her worth, was no longer found in what others said or how she was treated. She found her purpose the only way any

> She found her purpose the only way any of us can, through her encounter with God.

of us can, through her encounter with God. God came in and brought provision, healing, and restoration to Hagar. Her core beliefs about herself were changed through her experience with God's presence in her life.

CORE BELIEF ABOUT SELF

Our core beliefs about ourselves become damaged when we experience abuse as a child, especially continual abuse. Our core beliefs are the foundation and pillars of what we believe about ourselves, others, and the world in general. This is developed within us and is shaped by our experiences—positive and negative—our perceptions, words spoken over us, and our understanding based on our developmental stage in life. So based on these life experiences, how others react to us, treat us, speak to us, and our perceptions of the situation, all this affects our core beliefs about ourselves.

Let's take a deeper look at the foundations and pillars. The foundation is the core belief and the pillars are the thoughts, positive and negative, we believe based on that foundation.

Let's work on an example of this. In Erik Erikson's theory, the first developmental stage every person experiences as a child is the Trust/Mistrust stage. This is where we learn to trust others will be there for us, to care for us, and support us. This is the stage in which when we are infants, we cry, and our parents come and take care of us and meet our needs. If our needs are met, trust is developed within us. Throughout the growing up years, this stage can be affected beyond what we experienced when we were infants.

Let's look at a twelve-year-old girl I will call Anna who experienced continual sexual abuse in her home by her father from age seven until the age eleven. At eleven years old, she told a friend, and the authorities were notified. Her family did not respond well and accused her of lying. She later denied the charges after suffering from so much grief within her family system. In her time of need, she was betrayed once again. Mistrust became the foundation of her core beliefs based on the trust her father broke with the continual abuse and then, mistrust was confirmed by the way other family members treated her. Her pillars, her negative and positive thoughts, were established.

Anna now has a foundation of mistrust. She perceives situations in her life through that mistrust. What others say and do just confirm that others should not be trusted because they always betray you in the end. Anna is now an adult and has difficulty in relationships and friendships. She keeps everyone at an arm's length. She is sad her relationships don't always go well; she dreams of having that perfect love relationship and doesn't understand why she's attracted to those people who continually betray her. Anna's foundation is that of mistrust. Her thoughts confirm this, and she views others through damaged perceptions of self and her negative core belief system.

IDENTIFYING OUR CORE BELIEFS

To change our core beliefs about ourselves, we need to first learn to identify, understand, and recognize them and the power that they have in our lives. In order to do this we will use a therapy technique called laddering, which is found in the book, *Prisoners of Belief*,[24] where we ask ourselves two questions: "What if _____?" and "What does that mean to me?" Below you will find a series of questions as well as an example for most steps in parenthesis. This is a vital part to learning what our core beliefs are about ourselves and I encourage you not to skip over this section.

1. Think of a situation when you became angry, anxious, upset, hurt, depressed, or experienced another very strong reaction. Write it down.

_____

_____

_____

2. Based on that experience, write down what you were saying to yourself, your internal monologue, about the situation. (Example: "I can't believe she compared me to them. Am I that bad?")

_____

_____

Next, ask yourself, "What does that mean to me?" (Example: "It means that people see me in a negative way.")

_____

_____

Next, ask yourself, using the previous statement to fill in the blank, "What if_____? What does that mean to me?" (Example: "It means they don't like me.")

_____

_____

Next, ask yourself, using the previous statement to fill in the blank, "What if_____? What does that mean to me?" (Example: "It means others don't want to be my friend.")

_____

_____

Next, ask yourself, using the previous statement to fill in the blank, "What if _____? What does that mean to me?" (Example: "It means that no one loves or likes me.")

_____

_____

Next, ask yourself, using the previous statement to fill in the blank, "What if _____? What does that mean to me?" (Example: "I'll have no friends.")

_____

_____

Next, ask yourself, using the previous statement to fill in the blank, "What if _____? What does that mean to me?" (Example: "I'll be alone.")

_____

_____

Next, ask yourself, using the previous statement to fill in the blank, "What if _____? What does that mean to me?" (Example: "It means that I'm rejected and unlovable.")

_____

_____

You continue this process until you get to the core. Core beliefs are statements, declarations about ourselves. In this example, the core beliefs and triggers are about rejection and being unlovable. This situation wasn't necessarily about this, but when we follow the thinking process, we can get to our core beliefs and understand them.

Now, we do this every day of our lives. Somebody says or does something, and based on our core beliefs about ourselves, our foundation, and our thoughts, our pillars, it is confirmed to us. This does not mean that it is truth; it just means that this is our faulty thinking.

3. Write out your core belief statement (foundation) based on the process we just went through. (Example: "I'm not loved or likable, so eventually everybody will reject me.")

_____

_____

4. Next, using your core belief statement (foundation), look at the different aspects of your life listed below and write how this statement negatively affects each area. (Example: "I struggle with my perceived rejection by my boss if preference is given to others. I wonder what's wrong with me.")

Mood:

Relationships:

Work:

Play:

Faith in God:

Other:

IDENTIFYING OUR LIFE RULES

Every day we make decisions based on our life rules. These life rules are developed from our core beliefs and the rules we have established from them. In *Prisoners of Belief* we read, "These rules are a blueprint for how you need to act in the world in order to avoid pain and catastrophe. Behind each rule is a catastrophic assumption about how things will turn out if you ignore its mandate."[25]

As a part of the process of walking into a healthy place in our thoughts, we need to identify our life rules, both the positive and negative aspects of them, so we can begin to challenge our faulty core beliefs.

Using your core belief statement (foundation) that you wrote above, make a list of the unspoken or spoken rules you follow daily based on this statement. (Example: "Why put myself out there when people don't really want to be with me?")

Rule 1

_____

_____

Rule 2

_____

_____

Rule 3

_____

_____

Rule 4

_____

_____

Rule 5

_____

_____

CHANGING OUR CORE BELIEFS

1. Recognize and identify your faulty core beliefs (foundations).

2. Recognize your faulty thinking (pillars) based on core beliefs.

3. Change your thinking when situations happen and old, negative thinking comes. Replace it or reframe it to positive thinking. Give examples. Tell yourself the truth, not the distortions based on past experiences.

4. Replace your negative thinking with God's truth and Word. What does God say about who you are, your value, and your future? Gather those truths together and pray those Scriptures over your life.

Damaged Spirits

The first time I ever heard about Jesus was in the fifth grade. I remember sitting in the VFW Hall a block away from our school where we were listening to two older ladies (now they don't seem so old to me), share with me and others in the room about the love God has for us all. As the women spoke, I looked around the room at the faces of my friends and thought about the different things going on in their lives. I thought, *That is so wonderful that God loves them; they really need that.* Never did the thought occur to me about God loving me; I only thought of my friends. I couldn't understand or accept that love for myself, but I was oh so happy for my friends that God loved them.

At the end of the service, one of the women came and sat next to me. She gently asked me if I knew how much God loved me. I still remember my words back to her: "Oh, God doesn't love me, but I'm so happy for my friends here. They really needed to hear that." She replied, "God loves you, too." I wasn't able to absorb the thought that I was worthy of love or that I was lovable by anyone. So I stayed with my opinion that the love of God they were speaking about did not include me, but God loved everyone else in the room. I truly believed this thought, and there was no changing my mind. In fact, for years this was what I believed, but our God is loving and patient. He continued to show His love for me, and slowly I began to realize and accept that I was lovable, but I'm getting ahead of myself!

UNLOVABLE

Many things happened in my life in fifth grade. I had my first boyfriend, which lasted but a few weeks. My family had moved to town when I was in fourth grade, and there was a time of adjustment, but by the fifth grade, I had a group of friends. I experienced bullying for the first time because of the boyfriend. I dislocated my thumb playing tetherball, was the fastest female runner in my grade, and school was my favorite place to be. There were many wonderful memories about that time, and then there were the not-so-wonderful memories. I was introduced to a world that children my age weren't meant to know about. This was the year that two of my older neighborhood friends pulled me into their secret world of sexual abuse. I began to learn the lesson that love and acceptance involved sex. Thus, my distorted view of love was developed. My actions in the years to follow were through my desire to have love and acceptance, and my belief was that sex was how one truly felt loved.

OUR DAMAGED SPIRITS

> The greatest damage that comes to us is our perception of love.

These past few months, I've been focusing, studying, digging, and waiting on God for this chapter about our damaged spirits. In fact, this chapter has taken longer than any other to write. It speaks to me of the importance of being guided by the Holy Spirit in what I say.

A spirit becomes damaged by more than what we experience; however, what we experience creates such damage that it is difficult, if not impossible, to find our healing without God. I venture to say that most of us are damaged. Let me explain and refresh what we read earlier. The things I have gone through affect my perception of those around me, of life experiences, and of my opinions of others. My filters are not clean. This is due to living in a sin-filled world. Then abuse comes into my life. My perceptions are further damaged. More things have come in to clog the filter from which I view life. All experiences go through this filter. Thus, there is more damage to my spirit because of life experiences.

The greatest damage coming to us is our perception of love.

As you read the previous sentence, maybe your thoughts immediately went to, *But you don't know what I've been through. How could you say the greatest damage is my perception of love? What about what happened to me: the abuse, the pain, the suffering, and the memories?*

I realize your pain is real and your memories can be overwhelming, but please understand it is our concept of love, our ability to love and be loved, that is damaged the most by the abuse. This is the core of the damage to our spirit: our concept and perception of love.

THE WORLD'S VIEW OF LOVE

Love. What is love? In our society and world today, the word *love* has become distorted and corrupt. For many who have walked in similar shoes to mine, love becomes about what I can give to someone else. Love is about sexual acts. As a counselor, I see many children, teens, and adults who act out sexually in various ways to please the other person so that they can feel love and acceptance from them. They feed into the distorted view of love the world gives, and the cycle continues because they were trained this is how you show love. Perpetrators are experts in deceiving those they abuse; that is part of the grooming process. Special favors are given—a false sense of love—in exchange for sexual acts. Perversion is rampant, abuse continues, and those who have been abused once as a child are often then abused by others. It is not uncommon for an individual who has been abused to experience sexual abuse from more than one individual.

When you have experienced abuse, often love has conditions. In reality, this is the world's view of love. There are conditions and requirements to getting love; it is not given without conditions. You must give something first to get the love and acceptance we all desire.

GOD'S VIEW OF LOVE

God's view of love is much different. God's love is not about what we can do for Him. His love comes with forgiveness, acceptance, and no conditions. God turned the cycle around, and His love is about what He can give us. Jesus, His only Son, a part of Himself, was given, was sacrificed, so that we could have a relationship with God. God does not love us because of what we can give Him. God loves us because we are His. God's love is pure and clean and for many, it is hard to accept or believe we are worthy of this type of love, so we go back to old ways to find the familiar feelings of love and acceptance. We hunger for and crave love, but we look for it through unhealthy means.

> God's love is not about what we can do for Him. His love comes with forgiveness, acceptance, and no conditions.

God's love is the substance of what we all need. It is the balm of Gilead; it is the source of our strength, deliverance, and healing. The very thing we often put a wall up to ignore is truly what we need. As a child, teen, and young adult, I had a wall up to God's love. I did not feel worthy of His kind of love. I was dirty, damaged goods, and thus, unlovable. Many of you reading this can relate to what I am saying. It is difficult to understand or grasp this kind of unconditional love. However, what we need is God's love. His love is not the love that we know; it's not the world's view of love or man's love. Because of our hurts, because of the damage to us by the world's view of love, this distorted love, we have placed a wall to protect us from being hurt again, and rightly so. However, God's love is our protection, not the wall. We can't view God's love through the eyes of man's love because it is distorted and unclean. God's love is the river of life, our healing, and our everything. God's love is pure, clean, and requires no conditions to receive it. God's love is what we need.

How do we find this love? Or should I say, how do we accept this love? The very thing that has become our shield is blocking us from fully accepting God's love—our walls of protection. For many, if not most of us, our walls will not come down in one strike. Usually, it is layers and bricks at a time, coming down to where we learn to receive, accept, and believe God's love for us. For us to do this, to take down our walls, we need to understand what God's love is for us.

SUBSTANCE

Earlier, I made a statement that God's love is the substance of what we all need. What does this word *substance* mean? At the *Free Dictionary Online* website, substance is defined as:

1. that which has mass and occupies space, matter;
2. essential nature; essence;
3. gist; heart;
4. that which is solid and practical in character, quality or importance;
5. density; body.[26]

At *dictionary.com* substance is defined in part as: "that of which a thing consists; physical matter or material; form and substance." [27]

So through both definitions, we understand that substance has a form; it is often viewed as a type of mass that occupies space; it is matter; it is solid; it is practical in character, quality, or importance; it has essence; it is the heart; it has weight; it is dense; and it has body.

Now look at love as a substance, *the* substance. Love has form; love is a type of mass that occupies space; love is solid; love is matter; love is practical in character, quality, or importance; love is essence; love has heart; love has weight; love has density; and love has body. That is God's love. God's love is not what we had viewed as love. God's love is pure, clean, valuable, healing, restorative, generous, kind, and redemptive.

God's love has always been, just as God has always been. God's love took on the form of a man who became our Savior, Jesus. God's love needed nothing else for its existence; it is absolute love, just like absolute substance. The substance of God's love is the Trinity, and for us to embrace, understand, and accept love as a substance, we begin and end with God the Father, God the Son, and God the Holy Spirit. The fullness of God is the substance of love.

To receive God's love is to receive the fullness of God through the Trinity. Each part of the Trinity is a dimension of God's love. God the Father is the one who provides, protects, cares for, nurtures, disciplines, and mentors His children. He is our shelter, our strong tower, the I AM, our peace, our Creator, and all we need.

God the Son is who died for us and through accepting Him, asking for forgiveness of our sins, and letting Him into our hearts to change us, heal us, and restore us, we are reborn. Jesus is the Bridegroom, the chief cornerstone, the morning star, the Prince of Peace, the way, the truth and the life. There is no other way to the Father but through Jesus who died on the cross for our sins, and through Him we are redeemed, made clean, and placed in right relationship with God. He is the fullness of God's love, the substance of God's love, coming to earth and taking on man's form, to walk as we do so that we could be redeemed.

God the Holy Spirit is a gift to every believer. He is our Counselor, the Spirit of truth, and the Spirit of wisdom and understanding. He is the Spirit of knowledge and the fear of the Lord. He is the gift that Jesus said would be coming after His death and resurrection, a part of the Trinity that was sent to lead, guide, counsel, and direct all believers.

A MOMENT OF REFLECTION

Wow, I don't know about you, but just taking that all in can be overwhelming. It is a mouthful and so much to absorb. So let's go back to that little girl in fifth grade who was told that God loved her. She did not know or understand what true and pure love was. She was scared; she felt unlovable and unworthy to be treated kindly. How many of you reading this right now feel this way? You agree that God is love, and that is wonderful for your friends, but for you, not so much. Your wall is up, that wall of protection, that wall that has kept you safe for so many years. In fact, you wouldn't even know where and how to bring down your walls.

Let us start that process now. Let us stop and ask God, through prayer, to begin that work in us. Will you join me in prayer right now?

Dear God, Your love is but a scary thing to us. It is something that eludes us and is too much to grasp or understand. My thoughts go immediately to, *But if You knew the real me, You would see there is nothing to love.* Change our thinking this day, God. Help us to see ourselves through Your eyes, through Your love. Help us to not fear Your love, to not put our walls up to You Lord. Heal the wounds within us that stop us from being able to accept Your love. Open our eyes to see the truth, open our ears to hear clearly, and open our hearts to accept and receive Your love this day in our lives. Help us to understand these words we have read. May they penetrate our hearts and souls and allow another layer of hurt to be healed in us. We seek to know You, Lord, and not to fear You. Help us to do this. In Jesus' name, amen.

GOD'S WORD ON LOVE

To understand God's love, we must go to His manual for our lives, the Bible. What does God's Word say about His love for us?

I'm asking God to give you a gift from the wealth of his glory. I pray that he would give you inner strength and power through his Spirit. Then Christ will live in you through faith. I also pray that love may be the ground into which you sink your roots and on which you have your foundation. This way, with all of God's people you will be able to understand how wide, long, high, and deep his love is. You will know Christ's love, which goes far beyond any knowledge. I am praying this so that you may be completely filled with God. Glory belongs to God, whose power is at work in us. By this power he can do infinitely more than we can ask or imagine (Eph. 3:16–20 GW).

This Scripture tells us that love needs to be the ground in which we sink our roots and on which we have our foundation. Going back to our previous chapter on our core beliefs, we discussed foundations and that the pillars were our thoughts of ourselves. If *unlovable* is a part of your foundation, then your pillars are the thoughts, *God can't love me, The things I've done stop me from being loved by God or anyone for that matter,* or *If I give you something, then you will love me.*

This Scripture is telling us that *love* is the ground in which we should sink our roots, our foundation. God's love is our foundation, not our faulty core beliefs about ourselves telling us we are unlovable.

What else does God's love tell us about God?

CREATED IN HIS IMAGE

"So God created mankind in his own image, in the image of God he created them; male and female he created them" (Gen. 1:27 NIV). God created us in His image, and love is part of God. It is the substance of God. It is the essence of God.

A PLACE OF REFUGE

"How precious is Your steadfast love, O God! The children of men take refuge and put their trust under the shadow of Your wings" (Ps. 36:7 AMPC).

STRENGTH

"But I will sing of Your mighty strength and power; yes, I will sing aloud of Your mercy and loving-kindness in the morning; for You have been to me a defense (a fortress and a high tower) and a refuge in the day of my distress. Unto You, O my Strength, I will sing praises; for God is my Defense, my Fortress, and High Tower, the God who shows me mercy and steadfast love" (Ps. 59:16–17 AMPC).

COMPASSIONATE AND GRACIOUS

"But you, Lord, are a compassionate and gracious God, slow to anger, abounding in love and faithfulness" (Ps. 86:15 NIV).

DELIVERER

"But you, Sovereign Lord, help me for Your name's sake; out of the goodness of Your love, deliver me. For I am poor and needy, and my heart is wounded within me. I fade away like an evening shadow; I am shaken off like a locust. My knees give way from fasting; my body is thin and gaunt. I am an object of scorn to my accusers; when they see me, they shake their heads. Help me, Lord my God; save me according to Your unfailing love" (Ps. 109:21–26 NIV).

HEALING

"And hope does not put us to shame, because God's love has been poured out into our hearts through the Holy Spirit, who has been given to us" (Rom. 5:5 NIV).

REDEEMER

"This is how God showed his love among us; He sent His one and only Son into the world that we might live through Him. This is love, not that we loved God, but that He loved us and sent his Son as an atoning sacrifice for our sins" (1 John 4:9–10 NIV).

God's love is all of these to each of us. God's love is about what He has done for us, not what we have done for Him. This is different from the world's version of love that says we must do something to get that love. God's love provides a bridge to having a relationship with Him. The bridge is Jesus. This is what God wants from us: a relationship, but not in the way we have experienced bad relationships, relationships in the world. He will not abuse us. He will not use us and throw us away. He is not out for His own pleasure; instead, His love is protective, healing, compassionate, gracious, strengthening, redeeming, and a shelter to us.

A NEW UNDERSTANDING OF LOVE

Out of this new understanding of love, God's love, we pray for healing of our wrong definitions. We pray for God to change our understanding of love. When we embrace this new concept of love, we begin a journey that is much like going down a river and coming to a fork. Which side do we go down: the one that is familiar or the one that is of God's love? As we pray for God to change our understanding of love, we are naturally led toward God's love that leads to so much in our lives. Now, on this river journey, we come to a place that is bumpy and has some rapids. This is the place of forgiveness. This is the place where we learn to forgive ourselves, and for some, it is about forgiving God.

FORGIVING OURSELVES

It is very common for survivors of abuse to blame themselves or God for what has happened to them. When we blame ourselves, we are saying that we could have controlled or stopped what happened to us. Sometimes others have said that it was your fault, and you believed that lie.

The truth is we are still alive, and we did what we did to survive. We lived through a horrible experience, and we are not to blame. The most important thing we could do was survive, and that is what we did. We survived. We are alive. We are bruised and beaten up physically, spiritually, and emotionally, but nonetheless, we survived. This is the most important thought to cling to during the traumatic events.

Afterwards, we began to second-guess how we handled the situations confronting us. We began to believe the lie that we could have changed the situation or controlled the abusers. The truth is, our job at that very moment was survival, and that is what we did. When we put it into perspective and view it through the eyes of our role, which was to survive, then we can put the responsibility on whom it belongs, the abuser, and not on ourselves anymore. This begins the process of change in our thinking about ourselves. Then revelation hits us, and we slowly see that we are good, we are worthy, and we are lovable. Our old thinking begins to drop down into the river we are on in this journey, and we can see it drift away. As we embrace this new truth, we can accept God's love because we no longer view ourselves through the concept, the thought, that we are to blame, we are bad, and we are unworthy. As those thoughts drift away, God's love can come in and envelop us, and we are able to accept His love for us.

FORGIVING GOD

As Christians, we often associate the word *forgiveness* with Jesus who died upon the cross for our sins and in whom we find our forgiveness. The word *forgiveness*, in general, is looked at from two sides. The first side is forgiving someone for something they have done towards another.

The second side is letting go of blaming someone for something or a situation that happened towards another. The first is association with someone else's actions. The second is in relation to our perception of blame or responsibility—not always accurate, but perceived blame. For some who are reading this book, there is anger, hurt, and a lack of forgiveness toward God, who they perceive should be blamed, in part, for what happened. The thought has gone through your mind over and over, "If God really loved me, He would have stopped what happened to me." We have all heard others say, "If there really was a God, He would stop the ugliness in this world." This is hard to grasp, but from the beginning of creation, God has given man free will to choose. With the free will, man chooses to do good and chooses to do evil. God did not do these things to you, however, God can turn things around in your life and use what the enemy meant to destroy you to glorify His kingdom and bring restorative health and wholeness.

Please hear my heart. I am not saying, in any way, that God did this to you or allowed it. What I am saying is that man has a free will and God has honored that from the beginning of creation and has not crossed that line of taking it away regardless of the bad choices man has made.

Let's take a moment to look at free will to understand how it applies to us individually and to our situations. To understand it, we need to go to the beginning. In Genesis, chapters 1–3, we read about creation and the beginning days of mankind with Adam and Eve. In Genesis 1:27, we read how God created man in His own image, both male and female. I find it interesting that it took two, both male and female, to be created in God's image, which reflects on the Trinity and the relationships between God the Father, God the Son, and God the Holy Spirit. Created in God's image includes relationships, family, and community, which involve more than one.

In Genesis 2, we read about life in the garden of Eden and all God put in the garden. It says God planted a garden and made every tree in that garden. Two of those trees were the Tree of Life and the Tree of Knowledge of Good and Evil. God told Adam they could eat of any tree in the garden except these two, but if they ate of the Tree of Knowledge, they would die.

Right from the beginning, God gave man a choice. Just a few Scriptures later, Eve was deceived by the serpent, and she ate of the Tree of Knowledge and gave some to Adam as well. Now God could have come in and stopped them before they ate, but He gave them free will to make choices in their lives. He did not create them to be His robots and demand that they have a relationship with Him and worship Him. No, He gave them the *choice* to have a relationship with Him. Giving us choices, free will, wasn't just in one or two things. No, it had to be that man had a free will to choose in everything. It was and is an all-or-nothing concept. Thus, mankind will, at times, choose good and at other times, choose evil. This is hard to understand, but truly, to have free will to choose to worship, love, and build a relationship with God, means that I have a choice in doing good in this world or doing evil.

I often ask teens I work with, "Are you using your powers for good or evil?" The context in which I ask them this is that God has given all of us gifts and talents as well as places of influence. Every part of us has a positive and negative aspect to it. Look at the personality trait of determination. When we think of determination, we think of overcoming great obstacles and not letting anything stop us or get in our way, right? This is a positive personality trait. This is using our powers for good. However, just like a battery, each personality trait has a positive and a negative side to it. The negative side of determination is stubbornness. Stubbornness often can get us into trouble, cause conflicts, and hurt others. Stubbornness is about thinking only of yourself and not anyone else. This is an example of someone using their gifts, talents, and their places of influence for evil because self is all that is thought about and what feels good to self without thought of others.

So man has free will, and with it, man does good and man does evil. Free will can do amazing things in this world. Mother Theresa used her free will to help others in need. Abraham Lincoln used his free will to end slavery in the United States regardless of the great opposition he faced. Rosa Parks also used her free will to stand up to injustice, and she refused to move to the back of the bus despite the threat of harm to herself. Free will can also be destructive. Hitler used his free will to destroy, torture, and kill others. Pol Pot, former leader of Cambodia, used his position of power to kill his own countrymen.

God hears your cries and is here to mend, heal, and restore you.

In Genesis 4, we read of how Cain used his free will to kill his brother Abel out of jealousy. Throughout the Bible and history, we hear of stories of those who used their free will for good and those who used it for evil. Free will, just like the Tree of Knowledge, comes with the ability to choose good or evil.

So what does this free will have to do with forgiving God? It helps us to understand God and God's heart. God's heart breaks when His creation hurts one another. God saw this potential and He sent His one and only Son, Jesus, to die for us so that we could find forgiveness, healing, and restoration. When we understand that God does not violate man's free will, we have a better understanding of God. Man has a choice to accept God's love and salvation through Jesus, but many only live for their own wants and desires and for some, those wants and desires are filled with evil and sickness. They have believed a lie, just like Adam and Eve did when they ate of the Tree of Knowledge, and that lie has grown and become the center of their worlds. Evil, sickness, perversion, hatred, and ugliness are the center of the lies that those who choose to do evil with their free will follow. The choices that those who abused us made were just that, their choices; they used their free will to hurt and abuse others. They are using their free will for evil.

Forgiving God is about understanding who He is and the concept and gift of free will. God did not choose that you were to be abused. God's heart was broken at what happened to you. In Genesis 4:10, we read about God's broken heart for Abel after his brother Cain killed him. It tells us, "And He said, 'What have you done? The voice of your brother's blood cries out to Me from the ground.'" God hears our cries, and He justly deals with those who have done evil and wrong. We may not see it, but God deals with all sin, all evil, and He is a just God.

As we let this understanding of free will and of God's justice flow over us, we can begin the process of forgiving God. God did not do this to you. God hears your cries and is here to mend, heal, and restore you. Forgiving self and God are huge steps toward accepting God's love in your life. As you speak out your forgiveness, love begins to fill its place in your life.

> Forgiveness is not an emotion. It is a choice.

FORGIVENESS

Forgiveness is not an emotion. It is a choice. What do you choose to do regarding this issue, to forgive or not? As we learned about free will giving us the ability to choose, it impacts our forgiveness as well. Forgiveness is a choice. In Deuteronomy we read:

> See, I have set before you today life and good, death and evil, in that I command you today to love the Lord your God, to walk in His ways, and to keep His commandments, His statues, and His judgments, that you may live and multiply; and the Lord your God will bless you in the land which you go to possess. But if your heart turns away so that you do not hear, and are drawn away, and worship other gods and serve them, I announce to you today that you shall surely perish; you shall not prolong your days in the land which you cross over the Jordan to go in and possess. I call heaven and earth as witnesses today against you, that I have set before you, life and death, blessing and cursing; therefore, choose life, that both you and your descendants may live; that you may love the Lord your God, that you may obey His voice, and that you may cling to Him, for He is your life and the length of your days; and that you may dwell in the land which the Lord swore to your fathers, to Abraham, Isaac, and Jacob, to give them (Deut. 30:15–20 NKJV).

God not only gives our abusers a choice to choose good over evil. God also gives us a choice. God is calling us to choose life, good, and blessings. Forgiveness is a choice that benefits us, and a lack of forgiveness hurts us. When I live a life of unforgiveness, it affects me and my descendants. My anger, my bitterness, and my pain can be transferred to others, to my loved ones, my descendants. I see it every day in my workplace as a counselor, the bitterness and anger that are transferred from a parent to a child and so on. I also see the love, forgiveness, blessings, life, and goodness that are transferred from a parent to a child. I, just like you, had

> When I live a life of unforgiveness, it affects me and my descendants. My anger, my bitterness, and my pain can be transferred to others, to my loved ones, my descendants.

this choice in my own life. I could choose to let my unforgiveness, my pain, affect my children. Instead, I chose to heal, to do the work, to forgive so that I could have a blessed life, for not only myself, but my children as well.

When I think of unforgiveness, I think of Lazarus. In John 11, we read that after Lazarus and had been dead in the tomb for four days, Jesus came and said these words, "Lazarus, come forth," and out of the grave he came with his grave clothes about him. Jesus then said, "Loose him, and let him go."

We are much like Lazarus. We are wrapped in the grave clothes of death, evil, pain, and unforgiveness from what we have experienced, and we need to be loosened from them. We need to take them off and lay them down, never to pick them up again. Today, we need to remove the death sentence put upon us by the evil done to us and walk out our forgiveness of self, of God, and yes, even of that person who abused us. Forgiveness is not about them. It's not saying, "It's okay what you did to me." Forgiveness is saying, "I am cutting the ties of the abuse you did to me and the power they have had over my life. No more will what you did to me dictate my present and my future. This moment, this day, as I cut the ties of the control and power that you have continued to have over me years after the abuse, I am taking back my life, my present, my future, my purpose, and the reason I was created. I am taking it all back, and I am placing my life, my present, my future, my purpose, and the reason I was created back into the hands of God. No longer will evil dictate who I am, but now God will speak into my life, and good will speak of who I am."

As we do this, hope is restored; it is breathed back into us, and life takes hold once again. We are Lazarus; we are coming forth from the dead, and once again are filled with life, with breath, and with purpose. We are free. When we do this, we are free.

In her book, *The Hiding Place,* Corrie Ten Boom talks about finding the ability to forgive a former Nazi SS man who was one of the first actual jailers she saw outside of the concentration camps. While she was speaking after the war, she had a moment that was truly a crisis of belief when he came to her and reached out to shake her hand. She silently prayed, "Jesus, I cannot forgive him. Give me Your forgiveness." She then went on to say, "As I took his hand, the most incredible thing occurred. From my shoulder, along my arm and through my hand, a current seemed to pass from me to him, while into my heart sprang a love for this stranger that almost overwhelmed me. And so I discovered that it is not on our forgiveness any more than on our goodness that the world's healing hinges, but on His. When He tells us to love our enemies, He gives, along with the command, the love itself. It took a lot of love."[28]

Love is the key. God's love is the substance; the form of our healing is through it. God's love is the key we all need to find our restoration. Do we still have to sift through the stuff in our heads? Yes, we do. God knows that, and He and the Holy Spirit are at work in us to heal our souls. However, love is the soil in which we sink our roots, and as we do this, we ask for His help where we struggle to forgive. Do you see why the enemy tries so hard to keep us in unforgiveness? He does not want each of you to be free. Forgiveness is about your freedom, your healing, and your restoration. It's not about the abuser. It's solely about you.

> Forgiveness is about your freedom, your healing, and your restoration. It's not about the abuser. It's solely about you.

WALLS OF PROTECTION

Going back to the wall of protection we have created around us to protect us from others, from hurt, pain, disappointment, and so much more, let us look at the concept of the wall in a new light.

FALSE WALL

Our false walls of protection are made of bricks that represent many things. These bricks have names such as: anger, offenses, hurt, damage, pain, difficult experiences, abuse, circumstances, unforgiveness, to name a few. Let's stop and take a moment to reflect on what the names of the bricks are for you. Write them below:

_____

_____

_____

Now each of these bricks is held in place by mortar, which in the case of the false walls, is made with the lies of Satan. Satan takes partial truths and distorts them and infuses us with his lies that contribute to us believing what the false walls/bricks tell us. Which, in turn, causes us to build our walls higher so that we will be protected. But the very thing that heals us, which is God's love, is what we are blocking ourselves from accepting.

GOD'S WALL

God's wall is different from the false wall we have relied on for our protection. God's wall is made up of bricks that speak of who God is. Earlier, we read about some of those names: provider, protector, nurturer, mentor, shelter, strong tower, the I AM, peace, Creator, restorer, Savior, Bridegroom, chief cornerstone, morning star, Prince of Peace, the way, the truth, and the life, Redeemer, Counselor, Spirit of truth, Spirit of wisdom and understanding, gift, Almighty God! These are just some of the names of the bricks on God's walls of protection to which we run! The mortar of God's wall is God's love. Love seals the names and bricks in place in God's wall of protection. When we view these walls next to each other, I don't know about you, but for me, God's wall is what I want to protect me now, not my false wall.

In order for God's wall to become our protection, we need to remove the false walls in our lives. How do we do that? For many, this is something that you want, but it is also a very scary thought. At least you are familiar with the false wall. To embrace and accept God's wall of protection, we must let go of the false wall, the bricks, and the mortar that hold the wall in place. This is hard to do, but it is necessary.

REMOVING OUR FALSE WALLS

First, we need to apply the blood of Jesus to our circumstances through prayer. We need to pray and ask God to cover us, our perceptions, our experiences, our pain, our offenses, our hurts, and everything else with the blood of Jesus. As we pray this prayer, we need to also give God permission to come in and do the work in us, layer by layer, dimension by dimension.

Second, we need to read God's Word and seek out the Scriptures that speak of the truth of who God is and who we are in Him. I've given you a partial list of the names of God. Research and read about the many different names of God. Meditate on those Scriptures. Let God's Word breathe life into you. Next, read the Scriptures that speak of who we are to God. Pray these Scriptures over your life. Speak life into your dry and weary bones. Pray life and live like one who is living and not one who is dead like Lazarus before Jesus came.

Where are you hurting? What are the words that describe your current spiritual condition? For some, it may be broken, hurt, pain, rejected, or unloved. This will show us where your need is. Make a list of those words below:

_____

_____

_____

_____

_____

_____

Now that you have listed them all, go over your list and write down what is the opposite of that hurt. For example, if you put rejection, the opposite—your need—is acceptance. Go through your list of words describing your spiritual condition and write the opposite next to it. Remember, every negative has an opposite that is positive. The positive speaks of life and hope, and the negative speaks of death and despair.

Once you have established your list of needs, pray those needs and speak them into your life. May your prayer life shift from focusing on the rejection to acceptance or from pain to joy.

As you pray over yourself, speak life into your dry and weary spirit. As you do this, over time God will heal and take away the false walls in your life.

Finally, pray daily for God to help you accept and embrace His love in your life, in your past, and in all of you. As you do this, God will continue to heal and destroy the false walls and prayer will, in turn, become the mortar in God's wall, and He will become the protector in your life.

Restoration of Borders, Boundaries, and Pathways

First off, I want to say well done! You did it! You made it this far in the book, and my guess is God has made powerful and amazing changes in your life. You have been challenged, and God has brought healing to you in many areas. I am continuing to pray for you and believe God will speak to you and bring His complete restoration in this process.

As we begin the final section of our book, we focus on the journey of restoration. When I hear the word *restoration*, immediately my thoughts go to a piece of antique furniture. I absolutely love old pieces of furniture, really any type of antique, and in fact, many of them can be found in our home. Some of these pieces have taken work to get them to the place they are today. We found them, took them home, restored them, and now we get to enjoy their beauty in our everyday life.

The process of restoration is work. The pieces that need restoration are you and me, but we have a choice in the process. We can stay the way we are, or we can allow the work to be done in us. This is what the journey has been so far: allowing God to do the works of healing in our Soul Gardens. Now, an old piece of furniture can't get up and walk away, but we can and often we do just that.

A while ago I had a conversation with my spiritual mom and dad. They were complimenting me on the changes in me over the years. They have seen what I came from to who I am today. My response to them was, "I prayed a prayer way back that I didn't want to live a life as a victim; I want to live in the fullness of who God created me to be."

My spiritual father replied, "Kristin, many people pray that prayer, that's the easy part. The hard part is walking it out."

As I pondered his words, I was reminded of a book I read years ago written by Stephen Arterburn called *Healing is a Choice*.[29] This title is so true. I chose to stay on the workbench as the Master, our God, has done sanding, scrapping, hammering, and reshaping in my life. I've surrendered my flesh to the hand of God with a joyful heart even though, at times, the pain was great. I've committed my life to God; my will and all that is in me is God's. In return, God has done a great work of restoration in me.

In my surrender to God amid difficulties, trials, and pain, I have learned not to allow my circumstances to dictate my future, my life, my joy, or my peace. My circumstances haven't changed in many situations, but my response to them, for the most part, is no longer a reaction. As I have made the choice to be healed, God has taught me, and is still teaching me, to be a responder. One who responds as Christ would in any given situation.

Restoration is something we don't just pray about. It's a choice. It's a choice to change our thinking and our lives and to give up those things, thoughts, and lifestyles as God asks. We must let go of the things that block us from change. We can't get something new without letting go of what we currently have. We need to let go of the old debris, the rusted paint, and allow the Master to come in and restore us piece by piece, section by section, for that is what He desires to do in all of us.

Now we are beginning the journey of restoration. Let's go back to the image from the beginning of the book when we talked about a garden that had been destroyed. Imagine a beautiful, renewed garden with me. We have restored the plant areas and planted new life in the flower beds. We've worked on the lovely fountains, benches, arbors, and the broken places. Although we have done a great amount of work, there is still more to be done for our gardens, our Soul Gardens, for them to be fully restored. Our last section is about restoring our borders, boundaries, and pathways. Each of these must be restored for our gardens, our souls, us, to be fully healed and renewed into what and who God created us to be.

9

Borders

Restoring the borders represents restoring our relationship with Christ. In a garden, borders define and separate the plant area from the pathways. Stones are commonly used to define the borders to give clear boundaries to the area designated for the plants.

Borders represent our spiritual boundaries, insights, depth, and relationship with God. As our relationship with Christ grows, our spiritual boundaries grow and increase.

In Isaiah we read, "Enlarge the place of your tent, and let them stretch out the curtains of your dwellings; do not spare; lengthen your cords and strengthen your stakes. For you shall expand to the right and to the left" (Isa. 54:2–3 NKJV). This Scripture talks to us about our borders, the place of our tents, being extended. As we grow with Christ, He enlarges the place of our tents or borders, and our spiritual depth and insight grow and increase, which affects our relationships with Christ and with others because of Christ in us.

In Mark we read, "Wherever He entered, into villages, cities, or the country, they laid the sick in the marketplaces and begged Him that they might just touch the hem of His garment. And as many as touched Him were made well" (Mark 6:56 NKJV). This Scripture and Matthew 9:21 referring to the woman who touched the hem of Jesus' garment, both set a foundation of

> Borders represent our spiritual boundaries, insights, depth and relationship with God. As our relationship with Christ grows, our spiritual boundaries grow and increase.

Jesus as our border. When we reach out and touch the hem of His garment, we are changed. The hem of the garment is the border of the garment. It's what is around the edging. Borders in our gardens are what is around the edging of our plants, us, the spiritual fruit in our lives.

Jesus is the hem of us, the life in us, and the fruit in us. As we allow God to be in our lives daily, He brings His restorative power to our souls. We have talked in the previous chapters about God's love and how we were created to have a relationship with Him and one another. Now we are going to go a step further in our love relationship with God.

This section on borders is going to be a little bit different from the previous chapters. The first part of this discussion lays the foundation for the second part that is based on activities and interactions with God. It's about setting the foundation that Christ is our border, our cornerstone, and that our relationship with Christ is where the focus will be and not so much on our issues.

Two of the examples above discussed how people were healed as they touched the hem of Jesus' garment. They took their eyes off their issues and placed their full focus on Christ. As they did that, they were healed! If this is so, then as we reach out and touch the hem of Jesus' garment in our lives daily, He too will heal us and make us well!

CONVERSATIONS WITH JESUS

Building that love friendship or relationship with Jesus and beginning to hear His voice is part of the process of accepting God's love toward you. Often this is a place where many struggle. If you have had any abuse your life, your thoughts toward yourself are not always kind. In fact, they are usually critical and performance-based. This means that your love and acceptance are based on how well you perform for God and follow the rules, and often, you are motivated by man's approval. These are all areas we have discussed in previous chapters.

When we are in that process of learning to hear God speak to us individually, we need to remember that we often don't think kind things about ourselves. Then, we begin this journey of learning to hear God speak to us and often we shut Him down the moment He starts because His words are filled with love, kindness, and encouragement—they are uplifting, noncritical, and motivating words. We say to ourselves, "These couldn't be God's words about me."

> The still, small voice that tells us kind words is God speaking directly to us.

When we do these activities, these kind, loving words are God talking to us. The still, small voice that tells us kind words is God speaking directly to us. Some refer to it as our conscience, but even our consciences do not talk nicely to us about us. These kind words may go along the line of, "My daughter, I'm proud of you, I love you. You bring me joy; you bless me. My heart is broken for you. I see your heart and your tears, and I am here to help you, to be with you, to carry your pain."

These are not words that we speak to ourselves about ourselves. If you are an analytical person, you want to over analyze everything, to debate it. Refrain from doing that. You need to just write down the words, listen to what God is saying to you, and let those words penetrate your heart and spirit. Resist the urge to get caught in the debate, the sidetracking conversation of, "Is this God or not?" Remember, we rarely speak nicely to ourselves, and God is here to rebuild, restore, and renew us. When He is in the restoring process, edifying and encouraging words come to us. Just soak them up. Be a sponge and soak up God's presence and His words of love.

GOD'S WATER FOUNTAIN OF LOVE FOR US

As we establish our borders with God and they increase, we learn to trust. Our relationship with Christ is about a love friendship or relationship, and for many of us, a love relationship becomes distorted by the sickness in our world and how our world shows love. God's love is pure. God's love is not about perversion. God's love is so great for us that Jesus came and gave His life for us. Learning to embrace it is about restoring this belief system of pure love in the garden.

> The love has always been there; the only difference is that now we once again are embracing and open to God's love flowing in our hearts and lives.

As we discuss restoring the pure love relationship, let us imagine a fountain—you know, one of those three-tiered water fountains that sit in the middle of a garden. Imagine there is no water running in it. One day the switch is turned on, and the water begins to flow once again. It continually flows, always moving and never stopping. This is like God's love for us.

We can stop the love, though, because we don't want it or feel we don't deserve it. We don't want anything to do with God's pure love. It doesn't mean the fountain isn't there or that there isn't a spot for it, just as there is a spot in our hearts for God and God alone. As we bring back this fountain of life within ourselves, within our Soul Gardens, it's about love, God's love, being restored in us. The love has always been there; the only difference is that now we once again are embracing and open to God's love flowing in our hearts and lives.

RESTING IN JESUS

As a child, I loved floating in the water. There was something peaceful and freeing when I would rest my back upon the water with my face fully in the sun, feeling its warmth, my eyes closed, body relaxed in total surrender to the process of floating. My hands gently moved in the water and every part of me was relaxed and taking in the heat from the sun. This was about total abandonment and trust in the process of floating.

... as we surrender our wrong thinking to Him, we can embrace and trust Him and accept His love for us.

Trusting God is just that: learning to relax, releasing in His presence, absorbing from Jesus the Son in total surrender. There is something about the steps, the process of floating, that involves rest, surrender, and relaxing because if you struggle, if you are tense, if you are trying to cause it on your own, it won't happen. It's only when you lie back, release yourself, and become flat out that you are able to float. The head must be back in total surrender, it must be in a humble, flat position. Our mind, our wrong concepts are represented here. We need to transition from our wrong thinking to God-thinking. Restoring of our minds, our thought processes, are vital to the trusting God process.

In Ephesians we are told, "For we do not wrestle against flesh and blood, but against the rulers, against the authorities, against the cosmic powers over this present darkness, against the spiritual forces of evil in the heavenly places" (Eph. 6:12 ESV). Jesus came to restore, to transform our thinking, our thought processes, as we have already discussed. Now as we surrender our wrong thinking to Him, we can embrace and trust Him and accept His love for us.

It's about learning to lay our heads back, to close our eyes, and to tell God, "I trust You with these circumstances. I trust You with my life."

We want to struggle and do things ourselves. This trust, this pure love relationship is about learning to trust God. It's about learning to lay our heads back, to close our eyes, and to tell God, "I trust You with these circumstances. I trust You with my life."

God's intention for us is not to destroy us or punish us. God's intention for us is good. The beautiful thing about God is that He does not set us up. God is here to love us with His pure love, and in the midst of everything that we have been through, God loves us. God is here to love and restore us. God's love is a pure love, a clean love. It's a love that doesn't have a motive for itself. It's a love that would lay down its life for us.

ACTIVITIES

Join me as we focus on the hem of Jesus' garment and our relationships with God. This is a safe place and time to do this. May God bless you and bring great revelation as you journey through these exercises. They are meant to be stepping stones to bring you to a closer understanding and relationship with God. Each one is valuable, and I encourage you to press in and do each one!

GOD CONCEPT

If we have a history of abuse, control, or shame, we often have a concept of God based on extremes. There are two sides to this. The first is the rule side that says, "Follow all of God's rules; He's the boss; He will judge me if I don't do it right; and if I don't do it right, He won't love me." This is a performance- and law-based concept that I must follow the rules in order for Jesus to love me. If this is the side you lean toward, then you need to move toward to the love side.

The second side is the love side. You are full of God's love and grace, but often, those filled only with God's love and grace lack boundaries in their lives. Others often take advantage of you, wrong teaching can come in, and hurt feelings happen often. Boundaries, which we will learn more about in the next section, are just as important as being filled with God's love.

Is your relationship with Christ more about following the rules, being good, and being performance based? If it is, that means your focus on the love relationship with God needs to be developed to a greater measure. I encourage you to go beyond what is in this book and make time in your life to focus on just being with Jesus and not on performing for Jesus' love and acceptance.

This activity will give you a better understanding of which side you fall on, the love and grace side or the rule side.

Describe your view, your concepts of God. Below, write as many words as you can to describe God.

_____

_____

_____

_____

_____

Now with the words you just listed above, place them below under the category they fit best, either on the love side or on the rule side. There are no right or wrong answers. The purpose of this activity is to honestly answer the questions so you can identify which God concepts you need to adjust as you grow in your relationship with Christ and how you view God.

Love and Grace	Rule

PARTNER WORK

If you are doing this book as a part of a group, divide into partners. Take time to debrief and discuss this activity with one another. Discuss the words you wrote down, which side they fell on, which side is fuller, and what stood out to you about yourself as you did this exercise.

If you are not participating in a group, find someone you trust and talk to them about your God concepts. Choose someone you look up to, trust, and have allowed to speak into your life. It would be very easy not to do these activities; however, they are a key to the restoration process. I encourage you to do them and allow Jesus to speak to your heart.

WORDS ART PIECE

Create an art piece that describes your definition of God, who you know Him to be. This can be a collage, watercolor, pastel, colored pencil, or whatever type of art piece you would like to create. To begin the activity, pray and invite the Holy Spirit to be a part of it and ask for His leading in working through this process.

- Ask yourself: Who is God to me? When I think of God, I think of _____.
- Write all the words, images, and pictures that come to your mind on a piece of paper.
- Incorporate all the words, images, and pictures in this art piece.
- As a group, share your art piece with one another and discuss what revelations came to you as you were doing this activity. (Individuals, please share with your trusted friend.)

PRAYER ACTIVITY WITH GOD

Now that you have completed your art piece, spend time with God and ask:

- What area or areas are missing?
- What aspects of You have not been included?

Compare that to the list of names of the Father, Holy Spirit, and Jesus that were in a previous chapter or do research on the Internet to see what areas in your revelation and relationship with God need to be nurtured.

- Look up Scriptures for those areas and study what God's Word says about those attributes of God.

ENCOUNTER WITH GOD

Find a location that represents peace to you, a place where you can feel comfortable spending time with God. It may be a place in your home, outside in your garden, at the beach, by a lake, or in the woods. The important thing is to find someplace where you will not be distracted by others so you can spend time alone with God and write down what He shares with you. Allow at least thirty minutes for this activity.

1. Get settled into the place and get comfortable.
2. As you are sitting there, imagine that God comes, sits down, and joins you in this place. What are the words that Jesus says to you?
3. Write them down in your journal.

OUT IN NATURE

Find a quiet place out in nature where you can focus on the beauty around you. It may be in your yard, going for a walk or a hike, sitting at the beach, or sitting under a tree in a nearby park. Regardless of whether we live in the city or in the country, we can all find a place or objects that represent nature. Flowers, leaves, trees, grass, the sky, or clouds are all examples of what to study in nature.

- Get settled into the place and get comfortable.
- Take notice of what is happening around you in nature.
- Look at nature from all sides and perspectives.
- What is it saying to you about God or God is saying to you through it?
- Write it down in your journal. (Example: Looking at a leaf with many lines, one could see that God is a God of details, and He sees and knows the details of our lives.)

ALONE TIME WITH GOD

Put on a worship song and get comfortable. You may want to lie on the floor, sit in a comfortable chair, or spread out on your couch. Close your eyes. Don't pray, just allow the words of the song to penetrate your spirit. All you can say is, "I love you," nothing else. Spend time with God. It's not about doing this or that or your list of prayer needs; it's just about being with Him. Focus on just being with God and listening to what He is saying to you. After you have finished, remember to write in your journal all that God spoke to you.

10

Boundaries

Boundaries in a garden are the stone walls, the garden hedges, and the picket or wrought iron fences separating what is inside the garden from what is outside. When these are destroyed, everything that is outside now has free access to come in, and all that is inside moves out. There is no longer a clearly defined boundary line for the garden.

Imagine a beautiful home with a white picket fence all around the yard and attached to the home. Within this yard, it is very clear what and where the boundaries are. Within this yard, safety, security, and peace can be found. When sexual abuse happens, those fences are knocked down, and we lose our clearly defined boundary lines when interacting with others. The lines are gone and, over time, there is no sign they ever existed.

We need to restore and rebuild those boundaries. Boundaries in our Soul Gardens are about our relationships with others. There are several amazing books about this topic, and I recommend you read them, especially *Boundaries* by Dr. Henry Cloud and Dr. John Townsend.[30] I am in no way attempting to recreate what they have already done in a powerful way. I highly recommend that if boundary issues are something you struggle with, then by all means, please get this book to work on those areas.

In relation to our Soul Gardens, I would like us to look at boundaries from the focal point of restoring our voices. When abuse happens, our voices have often been stunted. Individuals with a history of abuse struggle with insecurities and difficulties in sharing their voices in appropriate and healthy ways as well as using their voices to speak up for themselves when others cross their boundaries. Interactions with others, things that come into our lives, the way others treat us, and the actions done to us are all areas in which we have difficulty speaking out.

> God gave us voices to speak, to interact, and to have relationships with others and sadly, many of us struggle to speak out on our own behalf.

We have been quieted, shut down by the abuse, and often we don't think or feel that our voices matter. These are all boundary issues. When we do speak out, it is often because things have built up inside of us and we react to others out of frustration and anger, or we isolate and hide ourselves from the world around us.

God's plan for us is to be healthy and whole in all aspects of our lives. God gave us voices to speak, to interact, and to have relationships with others and sadly, many of us struggle to speak out on our own behalf. There are three areas I'd like to focus on regarding our voices: learning to say yes or no, learning to speak, and learning to roar.

LEARNING TO SAY YES OR NO

In relationships with others, often those who have been abused do one of two things: Either they say yes to everything and harbor feelings of resentment or of being used, or they say no to most things and stay isolated and away from others. Both are fear-based reactions.

When I became a Christian, I so wanted to be loved and accepted by my new Christian family. Whenever leadership or fellow believers would ask me to be involved in something, I would almost always say yes. I didn't have the skills to be balanced in my life because I didn't have clear boundaries. Often I felt overwhelmed and frustrated, but I wasn't able to see that this was due, in great part, to my lack of boundaries.

After a few years of going around and around the hamster wheel on this issue, God spoke to me one day and asked me to write a list of everything in which I was involved. After I did, He then asked me to divide the list into two columns: things He asked me to do and things I was involved in because I couldn't say no. God then encouraged me to begin the process of saying no. Over time, with God's love and patience, I learned to say no in other areas. Feelings of guilt bombarded me, but God taught me that this was using performance to find acceptance. God was teaching me to not be performance-based in my relationship with Him, but instead, to be Spirit-led in what I was involved with.

Being performance-led comes partly from the abuse. It's part of the grooming process. I was trained by the continual sexual abuse that performance was about acceptance. If I do this, you will accept me and love me regardless of the perversion and abuse. The motivation of my heart was to be accepted and loved. With no clear boundaries, I lost my voice to say no because as a child who was continually sexually abused, I didn't have a voice to say no. As a teen who was sexually assaulted, I tried to say no, but then more physical abuse came in the assault. So once again, I learned to keep my voice quiet, which followed me throughout part of my life.

Many of you reading this would say that your story is different but similar at the same time. You struggle with saying no to others out of fear of disappointing them or hurting them. In that process, we miss the realization of how we could be hurting ourselves, overloading ourselves, and making unhealthy choices that have consequences in our own lives.

On the other side of this scenario are those individuals who say no to everything out of fear and anxiety. Fear tells them, "You can't do that. Something bad might happen. Protect yourself. Say no. Stay home and away from hurt and pain." Fear has isolated their world. For this person, establishing healthy boundaries is about stepping out of the isolation of home and protection and learning to trust God and others. It's about building relationships with people and not isolating themselves from everyone out of self-protection.

ACTIVITY: IN WHAT AREAS ARE YOU INVOLVED?

Regardless of whether you are a yes or no person, write a list of your areas of involvement as mentioned earlier. Once the list is completed, make another list of those things in which God is asking you to be involved. For the person who never says no, this is about learning how to differentiate between what God is asking you to do versus what you feel compelled to do because you don't know how to say no. Ask yourself these questions:

- Am I doing this because someone else needed me to and I was afraid or couldn't say no?
- Have I prayed about doing this, or did I do it to get someone else's approval and acceptance?
- Do I feel God leading me to do this?
- Is this something that is bringing me closer to Jesus?
- Am I neglecting God, my marriage, or family because of this activity?

For the person who never says yes, this is about making a list of those things God is asking you to do in this season in your life. Ask yourself these questions:

- What are the top three to five things I feel God leading me to do? Make a separate list of those with space underneath each one.
- For each one, write out the different steps or goals to become involved in that activity.
- Highlight one or two steps or goals you will focus on and give yourself a timeframe of when you will complete it.
- Once completed, go back to the list and highlight the next few goals that you will work toward. Repeat until the list is completed.

Once your list of what God is asking and nudging you to do for this season is completed, go to a leader, a safe person, or a friend you trust and share it with them. Ask them to join you in prayer as you pursue what God is asking you to do. Remember, this is about taking small, bite-sized steps in the process of change. Change does not happen drastically overnight. Instead, as we learn and grow in our trust of God, it happens in levels, much like climbing stairs. Today, all I am asking is that you take the first step.

LEARNING TO SPEAK

> Obedience to Christ is often that: doing what others may think is ludicrous and doing it with a humble and submissive heart.

As I sat in the office with the entire staff, I boldly, but quietly, spoke of what God was leading me, my husband, and our family to do. With a humble and submissive heart, I shared the changes God was leading us to take. This was the first time I had boldness to share what God was leading me to do despite what others' opinions may have been. My words were of love and brokenness, as a ministry I loved dearly and birthed was to be left, and we were to walk into the unknown of change.

As we pursue our voices, it is then and only then that we can establish another layer or level of boundaries with others. My husband and I heard God speak to us, and as we obeyed God's voice and leading, I learned to set a boundary in my life with other people. Previously, I would always defer to what my spiritual leadership spoke to me about my life. Please hear me when I say that this is not about being rebellious to leadership. This is about maturing in Christ to where He spoke to us and we obeyed, regardless of what others around us may have thought. Obedience to Christ is often that: doing what others may think is ludicrous and doing it with a humble and submissive heart.

While I was at a conference a few years before this, a friend was praying for me. She told me she saw me as a roaring lion who still saw herself as a baby cub. When I roared, it scared me, but God was going to teach me to see myself the way He does with the power and authority that He has given me. I was scared and timid to use my voice. As I think back on that, my thoughts immediately go to you, my reader.

I am you, the one who is walking through the process of healing and restoration.

I am you, the one who survived abuse and is pursuing wholeness in mind and spirit.

I am you, the one who questions if I can ever live a day, a week, or a month without the abuse being triggered in my life?

I am you, the one who is actively pursuing God.

I am you, a survivor, a lion, a mighty woman of God, for whom God has great plans.

I am you, the woman who was created for so much more than what her past says to her.

I am you, and you are me.

Dear reader, I pray that you hear this. God has so much for you, and you are that lion to whom God is saying, "It is time to roar; it is time to see yourself the way I do. It is time to walk in the authority and power that I have given you through my Son. It is time, mighty woman of God, that you arise and speak as I created you to do."

FINDING MY VOICE

How do I find my voice amid so many others? One day at a time. The process for each of us will look different, but the result is we learn to roar as God intends us to do. The first part of this process for me was speaking out about God's leading even though I suspected that others would not agree. The second part was when we moved to Washington State, and I went back to school to finish my bachelor's degree. Because where we lived was a great distance from most colleges, I chose to finish my bachelor's degree with online classes. God brought me back to a place where I was writing.

As I began to write my papers, my opinions, the things that were inside of me, others began to recognize my voice. They began to speak to me of my voice and the importance and weight that my voice carried. This was a new concept to me, and it took time to absorb it. It was during this process of my professors' words of life being spoken to me that my hidden dream of writing began to stir. I found a place to share my voice. Often, with shaky words, I would write. I would question myself and what I was writing, but I wrote, and I shared my voice. I interacted during our online discussions, and I found myself becoming stronger and stronger.

For me, writing and being in school was the place I began to find my voice. I began to discover me. Where is that place for you? What is your voice drawn to do? What are you passionate about? Find that thing and do it. Is it cooking? Is it talking with others? Is it giving? Is it writing or painting? Whatever it is, do it, for in that activity you will develop your voice and share it with the world around you.

LEARNING TO ROAR

When I graduated with my bachelor's degree, I knew my time in school was not yet done. My reasons for returning to school had to do with the fact that I wanted the training and tools to help others. To do that fully, I needed a master's degree in counseling psychology. I often tell my friends that God had me in an intensive three-year program of becoming whole and healthy, and I just happened to be blessed with a master's degree in the process.

Through getting my education, I learned another layer and level of courage and boldness to start sharing my voice with others. God started speaking to me about writing, specifically about writing this book. Now, although God spoke to me about writing, I had a choice as to whether I was going to pursue it and share it with others. I remember the first time I spoke to a friend about what I felt God was leading me to do. This was far different from previous directions God had taken me in the past. This was a proclamation of sorts, where I was opening myself up to others and telling them, using my roar, to declare what God was leading me to do. I was establishing a boundary in my life.

I shared with a couple of dear friends that I felt God was leading me to write, minister, and speak to women. I went to a conference, took an all-day class on writing, and shared my dream of writing with those in my work group. Each time I shared with others what God was leading me to do, I felt my voice getting stronger and stronger. I was careful not to let others' opinions steal my joy and God's leading. I established another layer of healthy boundaries with others. I then went a step further and gathered a group of friends for lunch, shared the vision God had given me, and asked if they would partner with me in prayer. I was beginning to see myself the way Christ did and was actively moving in that direction.

> We will roar as the mature lion and no longer see ourselves as the timid cub fearful of her own roar.

For us to learn to roar, we need to use our voices, no matter how weak they may sound at first! For each of us that will look different, but the result is the same. We will see ourselves the way Christ sees us and use our voices. We will roar as the mature lion and no longer see ourselves as the timid cub fearful of her own roar.

ACTIVITY: FINDING MY VOICE

To find our voices and to become comfortable with using them, we need to practice. This activity is about stepping out in that direction. For this activity, you will need a journal. Your assignment is to write in your journal every day. Your writing doesn't need an agenda. In fact, it's better if you just write something, anything once a day. Make a point to do at least one page a day, that's it! Remember, there is no right or wrong in this process. As you do this, you will find your voice. Those areas you are drawn to are what you are going to write about. Be sure to think outside the box.

Make a commitment over the next thirty days or more to write daily. Out of that writing, God is going to speak to you about you. Let it happen naturally and then notice the patterns of where your heart and voice are leading you.

11

Pathways

Restoring the pathways in our gardens is the final step in healing our Soul Gardens. Often, in building or restoring a physical garden, the pathways are the final step as well. In restoring the pathways, we must first take out the old to build or restore healthy new pathways. Taking out the old involves removing any stone, brick, grass, rocks, or debris that have blocked the pathway from clearly being seen or followed. I don't know about you, but there have been so many times in my life when I couldn't see that pathway clearly, and at times I was filled with hopelessness at the thought of my life and future.

Throughout this process, this book, this journey on which God has had us, the focus has been on removing the old. As previously mentioned, this represents our old patterns of thinking, old belief systems, and faulty core beliefs about ourselves. This is the work that we have been doing. Now we will begin the process of putting in the new foundation.

LAYING THE FOUNDATION

The first step is to level the pathway to make sure there are no holes or spots that can trip us. Sand is used in this process. Going into those small hidden places, sand fills up the space and creates a level pathway where there were previous bumps, traps, and unsure ground. This represents the Holy Spirit in our lives, filling up the unlevel places in us with the truth of Jesus. Over the sand, landscaper paper is laid so that no weeds can come up. During this study we have done great work in pulling out the old, and we don't want those faulty thoughts to come back and grow. We need to continually build our relationship with God and focus on who God says we are and not on what our faulty, damaged thoughts say we are.

Who we are in Christ is the foundation of our lives; it is our life's call. Our identities are found in Christ alone, and when that is established, our foundations are sure and strong. It's level and no weeds can come up. Who we are in Christ is our foundation. Scriptures tell us:

> Our identities are found in Christ alone, and when that is established, our foundations are sure and strong.

I am created in God's image (Gen. 1:27).

I am a child of God (1 John 3:1).

I am an overcomer, and God in me is greater than what I face in this world (1 John 4:4).

I am a friend of God (John 15:15).

I am raised up with Christ and hidden in Christ (Col. 3:1, 3).

I am alive in Christ (Eph. 2:5).

I am a child and joint heir of God (Rom. 8:17).

I am loved and chosen by God (1 Thess. 1:4; Col. 3:12).

I am accepted by Christ (Rom. 15:7).

I am set free through Christ (Rom. 8:2).

I am no longer a slave but a free heir through Christ (Gal. 4:7).

I am God's workmanship created in Christ Jesus for good works (Eph. 2:10).

I have access to God with boldness through Christ Jesus (Eph. 3:12).

I am a new creation (2 Cor. 5:7).

I am the temple of the Holy Spirit (1 Cor. 6:19).

I am the head and not the tail (Deut. 28:13).

I am healed through Christ (Isa. 53:5; 1 Peter 2:24).

I am strengthened through Christ (Col. 1:11).

God has a clear plan set for my life that is one of peace, hope, and a future (Jer. 29:11).

> No longer do we focus on what the old voices or recordings of past experiences tell us, instead, we stand on who God says we are.

I don't know about you, but when I read those words, I feel strength coming into my spirit. God's Word is our strength, and when we speak God's Word over our lives and in our lives, our foundation and core beliefs about ourselves change. No longer do we focus on what the old voices or recordings of past experiences tell us; instead, we stand on who God says we are. Our foundation becomes strong and sure. Our identities are in Christ alone. He is our cornerstone, our sure foundation. Nothing that anyone else says or does can change who we are in Christ, although many have tried to deceive us into believing that we are lesser than others. Who we are is set in stone and cannot be changed. I find so much peace when I focus on who I am in Christ, and regardless of what has happened in my life, none of that can change who I am to God and who He is to me.

A MOMENT TO REFLECT

This is a selah moment where we need to just pause, give thanks to Jesus, and meditate on who we are in Christ and what God's Word tells us.

THE DIRECTION IS OUR CALLING

The second stage of restoring or building our pathways is the direction of the pathway itself. The direction is our calling. The pattern or direction it takes is the calling or purpose God has created for each of us individually. Regardless of where our journey takes us, our calling, our purpose is the common thread found throughout our life's journey. This is the common thread going through our lives and can start as a child but is not limited to a specific timeframe.

Often, we lose sight of who and what God called and created us to be. This is when we allow our circumstances, situations, or difficulties in life to define us and what our calling is. Instead, we need to take a step back and allow the Holy Spirit to speak to us about our calling—what God

> Instead, we need to take a step back and allow the Holy Spirit to speak to us of who and what our calling is—what God placed within each of us before we were even born.

placed within each of us before we were even born. Jeremiah 1:5 and Psalm 139:16 both speak of God having our days spoken of; our lives declared, even before we were born. God created each of us for such a time as this, and the calling, the purpose was not that you would be abused by others, but that you would walk out in the fullness of who and what God created you to be.

This is probably one of the areas that is most difficult for us to embrace, to accept, and/or to pursue. This is the place where many of us sit down part way on our journey and never get back up to walk on the pathway, the journey that God has set before us. Thoughts of insecurities, of lack, of inability overwhelm us, and we allow fear to stop us. Memories of what happened to us decide what our calling is instead of God. Who and what you are meant to be is who and what the world around you, this time in history, needs you to be. Nothing is by chance. You are the voice, the expression of Jesus that your sphere of influence needs to hear and see.

To rediscover our calling, we need to rediscover ourselves—our true selves and not the one that our experiences have shouted into our ears, the one that God created us to be while still in our mothers' wombs. Before we can do that, let's stop and take a moment to pray and ask for God's help in this process.

> Lord, we bring ourselves before You right now. We ask that You would reveal Your truth and life to each and every one of us. Lord, as we press in to You, lean upon You, and learn to trust You, help us to uncover who and what You created us to be. Speak to us as we do these activities. Open our eyes that we may see ourselves the way You do. Holy Spirit, guide us, uncover those lost and hidden things that are within us, and help us to discover who and what we were created to be. Silence the voice of past experiences, insecurities, and the destructive lies of the enemy of our souls. Reveal Your truth and abundant life to us and for us all. In Jesus' name, amen.

Activity: Self Discovery

Take a moment to ponder these questions and answer them. In this exercise, take notice of areas that may have been lost or forgotten deep within you.

I feel strong when:

_____

I am completely absorbed when:

_____

As a child, I loved to do, daydream about, or reenact through play:

_____

I am really curious about:

_____

When I was a child, I just knew I loved to:

_____

These activities make me feel empowered and jazzed:

_____

What are those hidden dreams that I never or rarely share with others?

_____

What is the common thread I see in my life?

_____

If I woke up tomorrow and there was no fear, no obstacles, nothing stopping me, I would:

_____

Then what would my life look like?

_____

And what would I be involved in?

_____

And where would I live?

_____

ACTIVITY: BURIED DREAMS[31]

This activity is meant to be done quickly. Don't overthink it. Be spontaneous. Pick up your shovel, and let's do some fast digging to uncover some of those buried dreams!

1. List five hobbies that sound fun.

2. List five classes that sound fun.

3. List five things you personally would never do that sound fun.

4. List five skills that would be fun to have.

5. List five things you used to enjoy doing.

6. List five silly things you would like to try once.

ACTIVITY: TIME TRAVEL[32]

1. In your journal, describe yourself at eighty years or older. What did you do over the years past your current age that you enjoyed? What did you become involved in? What was your life like? Where did you go? How were you the expression of Jesus in your sphere of influence? Where did Jesus take you? Did anything surprise you? Be very specific and give details.

2. Now write a letter from yourself at eighty years or older to yourself at your current age. What would you tell the current you about your life? What interests or directions would you encourage yourself to pursue? What dreams would you encourage yourself to pursue? What obstacles would you encourage yourself to overcome and how did you do it? Write down anything else you feel is missing the eighty-year-old you needs to tell the current you about your life, your calling, and your purpose.

JEWELS OF GIFTS AND TALENTS

The final part of restoring our pathways is looking at what they consist of—the stones, rocks, and jewels that make up and decorate our pathways. These represent our gifts and talents—those God-given talents and gifts mixed with our personality and all of who we are that make us unique individuals. Others may have some similar stones in their pathways; however, no two stone patterns are the same. For some, the pathway is filled with bricks. For others, it may be stone. Others are made up of gravel, tile, wood, or glass beads. Each pathway has its own colors and textures that have special significance to the person it is meant for.

What are your gifts and talents? Below you will find some activities to help spur those answers.

As a child, I was good at:

_____

As a teen, I developed skills in:

_____

Things that come natural to me are:

_____

My favorite and strongest skill is:

_____

My second favorite and strongest skill is:

_____

My third favorite and strongest skill is:

_____

Below, circle what applies to you.

With information, data, and ideas, I am good at:

gathering or creating	managing it	storing or retrieving information
putting it to use	problem solving	researching
planning	evaluating and appraising	inventing or designing new ideas
computers	technology communication	organizing
memorizing details	working with numbers	

With people, I am good at:

one on one	verbal communication	motivating
coaching/mentoring	written communication	counseling
instructing	training	serving
speaking	supervising	speaking or writing expressively
singing	playing an instrument	acting/mime
resolving conflicts	leading	

With things, I am good at:

crafting/sewing/weaving	making/producing	cooking
skills with building	skills with growing	cutting/carving/chiseling
setting up/assembling motor	physical coordination	molding/shaping/sculpting
precision work with hands	precision work with tools	disassembling or salvaging
eye and hand coordination	dexterity with hands	finishing/painting/restoring
drawing/painting	sports/physical activity	decorating

Any other gifts or talents not listed above:

_____

_____

OUR IDENTITIES

A final word about our identities as we end this chapter. One of the mistakes we make is that we look outside of Christ to find our identities. The most common place we do this is in our gifts, talents, and calling. We think they will give us value and self-worth. However, when we try to find our identities in these things, then disillusionment and discouragement can set in.

In my past, I walked through those times. I doubted what God gave me: His gifts, talents, and calling in my life to do a variety of things. I was trying to find my identity in what I did and not in who I was in Christ, and that led to doubt. We often look to ourselves or other people for our value and self-worth. Our identities are solely tied to Christ; our identities in Christ are where we find our value and self-worth.

> I was caught in the lie that what I do, my performance, brings me value, not in who I am through Christ.

During that season when I was trying to find my identity outside of Christ, I started realizing what God was really asking of me was to lay down my perceptions, expectations, and interpretations of what those gifts, talents, and calling looked like in and through my life. I had a concept in my head that wasn't necessarily what God intended. I was giving it the authority to dictate my value and self-worth, when Christ never gave it that authority. When my gifts and talents were in a season of rest, then my value went down because I wasn't using them. Do you see the trap I was in? I was caught in the lie that what I do, my performance, brings me value, not who I am through Christ. My calling, the pathway that is the common thread in my life, does not give me my identity.

If you get nothing else from this chapter, may this be what penetrates your spirit. Your identity is found in Christ alone. It's not in who you are, in what you can do, or where you go. It is solely in Christ and Christ alone.

12

Final Words

JOSEPH

In Genesis, we read about Joseph and the many obstacles or barriers he faced in his lifetime. God spoke to Joseph about His plans, but then it seemed that God's plan was interrupted. Tragedy happened. Joseph was kidnapped and betrayed by his own family, sold into slavery, false accusations were made against him, and then he was put in jail and forgotten. However, God's will and plans reign. Even in the midst of it when it appeared to Joseph that he was forgotten, God did not forget. God's plan appeared to be interrupted, but God redeems those tragedies in our lives. He covers them with the cleansing power of Jesus. Joseph had some huge barriers in his life, and he had a choice to let those barriers stop him or to move forward regardless of what he might face. Joseph could have given up, but he continued to move forward in the midst of his great pain. He chose to press in to God, Abba Father, to pursue Him despite the situation. Doors opened and doors shut. Finally, one day the doors opened, and he was taken out of prison and put in a position of leadership.

> What the enemy meant to use to destroy us, if not physically, then emotionally, mentally, and spiritually, is not the final say in our lives.

What the enemy meant to use to destroy us, if not physically, then emotionally, mentally, and spiritually, is not the final say in our lives. The Lord turns it around for His glory, and that was exactly what happened in Joseph's life. There was the moment when Joseph realized the fullness

> God's plan for each of us will go forward despite the tragedies and abuse we have experienced.

of what God had been doing in his life. When he saw his brothers again, he realized the Lord had turned this situation around for His glory, and he was exactly where God wanted him to be.

The plan for Joseph's life was not stopped, as it may have appeared. God's plan went forward despite the tragedies he faced. God's plan for each of us will go forward despite the tragedies and abuse we have experienced.

I believe in you. I believe in you walking out the fullness of who and what God created you to be. I believe in restoration in and for you. I believe that you are valued. I believe in you, but most importantly, God believes in you! I pray as you finish this book, this study, that you are walking away healed and restored, and I pray these Scriptures over each and every one of you:

May the Lord bless you and keep you [protect you, sustain you, and guard you]; *May* the Lord make His face to shine upon you [with favor], and be gracious to you [surrounding you with lovingkindness]; *May* the Lord lift up His countenance (face) upon you [with divine approval], and give you peace [a tranquil heart and life]. (Num. 6:24–26 AMP)

I pray that God would grant you according to the riches of His glory, to be strengthened with might through His Spirit in *your* inner man, that Christ may dwell in your hearts through faith; that you, being rooted and grounded in love, may be able to comprehend . . . what is the width and length and depth and height—to know the love of Christ which passes knowledge; that you may be filled with all the fullness of God. Now to Him who is able to do exceedingly abundantly above all that we ask or think, according to the power that works in you, to Him be the glory . . . in Jesus' name, amen. (Eph. 3:16–21 NKJV emphasis added)

Notes

Chapter 2 Our Soul Gardens

1   James Strong, Strong's Exhaustive Concordance of the Bible, (Iowa Falls, IA: World Bible Publishers, 1986).

2   Watchman Nee, The Spiritual Man, (New York, NY: Christian Fellowship Publishers, Inc., 1968), 27.

3   Joyce Meyer, Battlefield of the Mind, (Tulsa, OK: Harrison House, 1995).

4   Judson W. Van De Venter, "I Surrender All," (1896), http://www.hymnary.org/text/all_to_jesus_i_surrender.

Chapter 3 Vines of Shame

5   "Shame," Merriam-Webster.com. Merriam-Webster, n.d. Web. May 10, 2016, http://www.merriam-webster.com/dictionary/shame.

6   Lynn Heitritter and Jeanette Vought, Helping Victims of Sexual Abuse, (Minneapolis, MN: Bethany House, 1989, 2006), 146–147.

7   Donald L. Nathanson, The Many Faces of Shame, (New York, NY: The Guildford Press, 1987), 4.

8   John Bradshaw, Healing the Shame That Binds You, (Deerfield Beach, FL: Health Communications, Inc., 2005), 21.

9   Liberty Savard, Shattering Your Strongholds, (Gainesville, FL: Bridge-Logos Publishers, 1992).

Chapter 4 Weeds of Fear, Anxiety, and Control
10 "Weed of the Month: Liverwort," PennState Extension: Green Industry, http://extension.psu.edu/plants/green-industry/news/2012/weed-of-the-month-2013-marchantia-polymorpha-liverwort.
11 Timothy R. Jennings M.D., "Healing the Mind," 2008, DVD.
12 "Fear," Merriam-Webster.com. Merriam-Webster, n.d. Web. May 10 2016, http://www.merriam-webster.com/dictionary/fear.
13 Elyse Fitzpatrick, Overcoming Fear, Worry, and Anxiety, (Eugene, OR: Harvest House Publishers, 2001), 14.
14 Reginald Klimionok, Overcoming the Giants in Your Land, (Shippensburg, PA: Treasure House, 1982, 1986, 1987, 1992), 23.
15 Carol Kent, Tame Your Fears: And Transform Them into Faith, Confidence, and Action (Colorado Springs, CO: Navpress Publishing Group, 1993), 25.
16 Reneau Z. Peurifoy, MA, MFCC, Overcoming Anxiety: From Short-Term Fixes to Long-Term Recovery, (New York, NY: Holt Paperbacks, Henry Holt and Company, LLC, 1997), 7.
17 American Psychiatric Association, Diagnostic and Statistical Manual of Mental Disorders: DSM-IV-TR (4th ed., text rev.), (Washington, DC: American Psychiatric Association, 2000).
18 William Backus and Candace Backus, Untwisting Twisted Relationships, (Minneapolis, MN: Bethany House Publishers, 1988), 137.
19 Ibid., Peurifoy, 36.

Chapter 6 Damaged Emotions
20 "Chaos," Merriam-Webster.com. Merriam-Webster, n.d. Web, May 10. 2016, http://www.merriam-webster.com/dictionary/chaos.
21 "Chaos," American Heritage® Dictionary of the English Language, Fifth Edition. Copyright © 2011 by Houghton Mifflin Harcourt Publishing Company. Published by Houghton Mifflin Harcourt Publishing Company. All rights reserved, http://www.thefreedictionary.com/chaos.
22 Ibid., Strong, 8414.

Chapter 7 Damaged-Goods Thinking
23 "Shatter," American Heritage® Dictionary of the English Language, Fifth Edition. Copyright © 2011 by Houghton Mifflin Harcourt Publishing Company. Published by Houghton Mifflin Harcourt Publishing Company, All rights reserved, http://www.thefreedictionary.com/shattered.
24 Matthey McKay, PhD, and Patrick Fanning, Prisoners of Belief, (Oakland, CA: New Harbinger Publications, Inc.), 35–49.
25 Ibid., 79.

Chapter 8 Damaged Spirits

26 "Substance," American Heritage® Dictionary of the English Language, Fifth Edition. Copyright © 2011 by Houghton Mifflin Harcourt Publishing Company. Published by Houghton Mifflin Harcourt Publishing Company. All rights reserved. http://www.thefreedictionary.com/substance.

27 "Substance," (n.d.), Dictionary.com Unabridged. Retrieved May 4, 2016, from Dictionary.com website http://www.dictionary.com/browse/substance.

28 Corrie ten Boom, The Hiding Place, (Uhrichsville, OH: Barbour Publishing, Inc, 1971), 231.

Part 4 Restoration of Borders, Boundaries, and Pathways

29 Stephen Arterburn, Healing Is a Choice, (Nashville, TN: Thomas Nelson, Inc., 2005).

Chapter 10 Boundaries

30 Dr. Henry Cloud, and Dr. John Townsend, Boundaries, (Grand Rapids, MI: Zondervan, 1992).

Chapter 11 Pathways

31 Julia Cameron, The Artist's Way: A Spiritual Path to Higher Creativity, (New York, NY: Penguin Putnam Inc.) 86, 89.

32 Ibid.

What people are saying about
Healing for our Soul Gardens

In *Healing for our Soul Gardens*, Kristin Clouse transparently weaves elements of her own painful past together with proven and practical tools for helping others move from victim to victor. Kristin is theologically and psychologically sound in her approach and she offers exercises throughout the work to help the reader address his or her own pain. During my initial reading, I began thinking of friends and clients I am confident this book will help. *Healing for our Soul Gardens* is a moving and helpful book for anyone who has experienced pain and hurt.

—Kent Mankins, Ph.D., M.Ed., L.M.H.C., N.C.C.
Lead Pastor, Valley Assembly, Spokane Valley, WA

Reading *Healing for our Soul Gardens* is an unforgettable journey. Kristin skillfully offers compassion and hope for those impacted by the tragedy of abuse. The interactive activities are engaging and intentionally lead the reader through the process towards emotional wholeness. Having survived sexual abuse as a child myself, Healing for our Soul Gardens is a must read for anyone ready for a soul-changing experience!

—Beth Backes, Director of Pastoral Care for the
Northwest Ministry Network of the Assemblies of God

As a licensed counselor, a Christian and someone who has walked the road to healing, I wholeheartedly appreciate Kristin's bravery and vulnerability in tackling the overwhelming subject of sexual abuse. She welcomes you into her world—her hurts, pains and fears—and walks alongside you on your journey down the path of healing and restoration to wholeness. This book is comprised of heart-wrenching experiences coupled with the incredible grace and mercy of Jesus. Kristin's faith and training as a counselor aid her in helping you rediscover who you are at your core and open yourself up to allow God to speak His truth and love into your life. I highly encourage you to fully dive in and welcome all she has to say.

—Macee Whatley, Licensed Mental Health Counselor

I had the privilege and honor of going through the *Healing for our Soul Gardens* book with women from our congregation. As a women's ministry leader, being able to have a tool like this that can walk women through the pain of sexual abuse from a place of compassion and understanding to a destination of freedom and healing is immeasurable! I would without hesitation recommend this book study to any women's ministry leaders who desire to address a real and prevalent hurt that the Church has very often been silent in speaking to. Kristin's heart and voice resound in every chapter and its full of vulnerability and insights that can only come from what God does in a life when He takes the broken and makes it beautiful.

—Denise Vaughan, Rochester Life Women's Ministry Leader

Healing for Our Soul Gardens brings gently and directly a path for a changed future for the wounded parts of our souls. The use of the garden metaphor brings a visual and clarity to the effects of abuse I have not seen in the other books I have read on this subject. The detail of each emotion allows the reader to grasp how the abuse has changed them. However, Kristin effectively does not leave the reader with only empathy, but weaves throughout the pages of her book the path to freedom that will allow true healing. Kristen Clouse's activities in the book are especially helpful in experiencing healing that will last. I specialize in treating clients that have been victims of trauma and especially sexual abuse I definitely believe Kristin Clouse's book *Healing for Our Soul Gardens* would benefit my clientele in particular but it is written broadly enough for application to other issues.

—Ruth Graham MA, Licensed Mental Health Counselor

About the Author

Kristin Clouse is a author, counselor, speaker, teacher, mentor and leader to women. She has a BS in applied psychology from City University, and a MA in counseling psychology from Saint Martin's University. Currently in private practice as a licensed counselor, she works with children, teens, and adults who have experienced trauma and abuse, as well as other life issues. She blogs through Her Voice blog, of the Assembly of God Church, NW Ministry Network, as well as her own blog which can be found at KristinClouse.com.

Kristin's story is one of redemption, healing and restoration. As a child and teen she experienced sexual abuse in multiple situations and then she turned to drugs and alcohol to cope. As a young adult, she had a life changing encounter with Jesus, her Savior, and her life was forever changed.

She is a wife and a mother of two adult children, all of whom she absolutely adores. She is passionate about seeing women find freedom, healing and restoration in their own lives. She is the founder of The Restore Movement and Restore Ministries which both focus on finding healing from a variety of life issues and difficulties. She is a storyteller and uses allegorical examples to impart life, freedom, and healing to many. She speaks on a variety of topics at retreats, conferences, and workshops.

Kristin feels the call, passion, and purpose in her life to walk with others through life difficulties into God's plan for each of them. God has healed her, restored her, and raised her to walk into who and what He created her to be. God is the great Counselor and Physician and He truly can turn all things around for His glory! Her story is proof of this.

Learn more about Kristin at:

KristinClouse.com

Order Information

To order additional copies of this book, please visit
www.redemption-press.com.
Also available on Amazon.com and BarnesandNoble.com
Or by calling toll free 1-844-2REDEEM.

CPSIA information can be obtained
at www.ICGtesting.com
Printed in the USA
LVHW02s0556060318
568774LV00004B/4/P